W9-BDV-602

SKINHEAD
CONFESSIONS

SKINHEAD
CONFESSIONS

from Hate *to* Hope

T J LEYDEN
with
M. BRIDGET COOK

Sweetwater Books
Springville, Utah

© 2008 TJ Leyden with M. Bridget Cook

All rights reserved.

No part of this book may be reproduced in any form whatsoever, whether by graphic, visual, electronic, film, microfilm, tape recording, or any other means, without prior written permission of the publisher, except in the case of brief passages embodied in critical reviews and articles.

ISBN 13: 978-1-59955-133-3

Published by Sweetwater Books, an imprint of Cedar Fort, Inc., 2373 W. 700 S., Springville, UT 84663
Distributed by Cedar Fort, Inc., www.cedarfort.com

Cover design by Nicole Williams
Cover design © 2008 by Lyle Mortimer

Printed in the United States of America

10 9 8 7 6 5 4 3 2 1

Printed on acid-free paper

CONTENTS

ACKNOWLEDGMENTS IX

FOREWORD XI

PREFACE XV

1 Forged in Fury 1

2 Playing the Pawn........................... 13

3 Setting the Stage for Rage 19

4 Rapid Escalation........................... 27

5 Sudden Enemy 35

6 Rising Force 47

7 The Heat Is On............................ 55

8 The Few, the Proud, the Skinheads among the Marines ...65

9 Aryan Warrior and Bride Prepare for Battle 81

10 Hook, Line, and Sucker: Effective Recruiting Tactics 91

11 Blood Is Thicker Than Water 99

12 Drugs, Deception, and Disillusionment 107

13 One Step Forward, Two Steps Back 113

14 *Gullah Gullah Island* and Other "Color-ful" Tales.............. 119

15 Nature versus Nurture........................ 133

16 Cleansing Ethnic Hatred...................... 141

17 Fraternizing with the Enemy 149

18   180 Degrees—and Hotter 153

19   Redemption—From Hate to Hope 161

20   Second Chances 175

21   The Hand that Rocks the Cradle 181

22   Tolerance: The Only Bandage for the Hatred Sore 187

23   What You Don't Know Can Kill 189

APPENDIX 197

PICTURES 201

TJ LEYDEN

I would like to dedicate this book to my family.

To Julie, my sweets: Thank you for believing in me and
giving me the courage to do everything. I love you.

To my five men, Tom, Konrad, Brendon, Bailey, and Gavyn:
Thank you for letting me be your dad, father, and friend.

To my mother, who never gave up on me, even in my deepest, darkest hours.

I would like to thank all those who had a major impact in my life:
Julie Leyden, Thomas Leyden Sr., Sharon Leyden, Phil Leyden, Mat Leyden,
Dale Jensen, Jeff Mosley, and David Lazzar.

I would like to thank my friends who helped with the editing,
Jeff Mosley, Terrie Boyce, and Josh Richling, for all their help with the book,
as well as Karen Bastow, who assisted Bridget in editing.

To my coauthor, Bridget Cook, with special thanks,
for without her, this book would have never gotten started or finished.

BRIDGET COOK

To Val, BreeAnna, McKenzie, and Brent,
for always believing in me. You are priceless. I love you more than life.

To Mom and Dad, who opened my eyes to the wondrous world of humanity
and the divine within each of us.

To Lisa, Sarah, Kevin, Tab, Michelle, Mary Ellen, Tom, Barbie, Doug, Yvette,
Jan, Dwight, Dimitri, Angela, John, Chris, Vicki, Dan, Cherrie, Rick, Annie,
Peggy, Darryl, Ruth, Keryl, Cathie, and nameless others.

My love and deepest gratitude for all you have done.
Thank you, thank you, thank you!

FOREWORD

You've got to be taught to hate and fear,
You've got to be taught from year to year,
It's got to be drummed in your dear little ear
You've got to be carefully taught.

You've got to be taught to be afraid
Of people whose eyes are oddly made,
And people whose skin is a diff'rent shade,
You've got to be carefully taught.

—SOUTH PACIFIC

NO ONE, NOT one single soul, was ever born into this world filled with hatred for another soul or group of souls. And yet, we live in a world filled with hatred, filled with anger, and filled with terror. Where does it come from? How does it fester? How does it propagate?

We have all, at one time or another, found ourselves hating. We hate a bully. We hate a sibling or a parent or a spouse. We hate someone in power. We hate those who have done us wrong. But the searing quality of hate causes it to most often dissipate quickly. It takes enormous energy to hate. It is a fire that requires constant fueling. Otherwise it burns itself out, consuming itself and leaving only the harmless remnants. It is not a natural state.

But for some, it becomes a very natural state. It energizes. It provides purpose and direction. It comforts and justifies. It ennobles. The cost is only humanity—the natural connection and sense of community with all other people. And for some, that cost is worth it.

I never knew TJ Leyden when he was consumed by hatred. I never knew the angry, bitter, vicious creature he had been. Even though the first time we met he was still covered in ugly, racist tattoos from his jawline to his beltline, I could only see the hurt and desperate man he had been and the courageous, noble man he was becoming. His voice and demeanor were gentle and intelligent. He spoke of his love for his mother and siblings and for his sons from whom he was separated. He spoke honestly of his guilt and shame and his struggle to move beyond them and regain his humanity. I knew he was a marked man with a price on his head, yet he showed no signs of fear or even concern. I was charmed by him. I was proud of him. And I was inspired by him.

But I was meeting him on the far side of a journey through hell. For most of his adult life, he had been a very different human being. He had submerged himself into a world in which hate and the promise of violence and destruction were supreme. He only associated with those of like mind and intent. He had removed himself from family and friends and most of decent society. He espoused hate. He organized hate. He targeted victims based on his hatred and targeted sympathizers whom he could proselytize to and convert.

The story of what turned an intelligent, happy young teenager into a neo-Nazi white supremacist is fascinating in that it was not a single catastrophic event but a series of almost imperceptible shifts of circumstance and reaction that created the ruinous path. It is amazing to understand how violence, which would normally cause reprehension, could suddenly provide sustenance. It is remarkable to be privy to a whole community in which a central philosophy of hate motivates all activity. And it is compelling to see how easily that hatred can be focused and manipulated by those who seek to profit from it.

TJ will share that journey with you. But, more important, it is the story of his reconnection to his true self and the courageous struggle to heal. It is that journey that makes TJ a hero to me. I define a hero as one who perseveres and prevails despite enormous obstacle and despair. TJ is that, and more. What he has endured, what he has faced as he has taken back his life, is more than most of us will ever confront in our lives. It therefore serves as great inspiration to me as I face the far more trivial challenges of my own life.

But that alone still might not have earned my ringing endorsement of TJ's story. What has really become the most amazing result of his journey is his current work as a teacher and counselor. His ability to connect with young people and distraught people is profound, empowering them to take responsibility for themselves. His story has served as a great lesson for thousands of those who might have fallen victim to the same instincts that almost destroyed him. He has been saving lives for as long as I know him. He has been helping those of us who cannot comprehend it to understand what truly happens in the hearts and minds of those who hate. And with that understanding comes the ability to confront it and, hopefully, change it.

Like most of the great teachers in history, TJ has lived through a crisis of faith and has survived both enriched and inspired. And as a result, he is enriching and inspiring others. His story is not always pretty, but it is vital. This is a great cautionary tale and an epic story of how amazing the true spirit of humanity can be. It needs to be carefully taught.

TJ, I am so proud of you. You make me believe the best about our fellow men even when it is difficult to do so. So tell your children from me, their father is a giant and a hero. Thank you for the gift that lies between the covers of this book. May those who need it most find their way to it. God bless you.

Your friend,
Jason Alexander

PREFACE

I HEARD THE gasp of horror and knew I'd been caught. For several years I had hidden the depth of my involvement in the Skinheads from my parents, covering up my tattoos with long shirts, concealing my violent life through lies and deceit. Until now, my own mother hadn't known how far I was entrenched in the world of hate.

"What are those?" she cried, pointing at my body, which was covered from my neck to the middle of my back in graphic, sinister tattoos. "Tell me or I will call the police!"

No way in hell I was going to tell her what they meant—the hate crimes I had committed, the people I'd hurt, stabbed, and maimed to earn those tattoos. No way would I tell her about the hundreds of kids I'd initiated to follow me into the White Power Movement and the things they did for me every day.

She picked up the phone, her eyes locked on mine. They connected her to the gang unit of the Redlands Police Department. She questioned the officer about what she had seen, and her eyes grew bigger in disbelief. I showed no emotion, even as he told her that the person she was talking about must be a fully indoctrinated and active Skinhead. Then . . . the inevitable question. Did she personally know the dangerous person with the tattoos?

"It's my son, TJ Leyden," she admitted, her lips trembling. Hot tears of shame, frustration, and panic were running down her cheeks.

"You're kidding, right?" the cop said incredulously. "Is this a prank?" The officer proceeded to tell her that not only was I a part of the local gang of Skins called American Firm, but that I was an active recruiter, bringing in new people under me all the time—teaching them how to fight, how to hate.

"What I'm telling you is that your son is a powerful leader of one of the most dangerous gangs of Skinheads in the nation."

As I look back on my life as a Skinhead, I'm not sure that anyone could be more evil than I was. I also know that change is totally possible, for anyone. I always tell the kids I speak with, "If I can do it, I know you can do it. You never have to be stuck. You can always be more than you ever dreamed."

My mission is to bring more and more people to the truth that tolerance itself can be a way of life, a way of thinking and doing and being. I love to motivate and inspire kids to become more than what they think they are capable of. I like to motivate law enforcement groups to learn, understand, and watch for signs of hate groups and put a stop to them, as well as provide tolerance education in areas it is desperately needed. I love teaching the military how to erase the horrid stench of racism from their ranks and continue to walk the talk of tolerance. I love bringing the tolerance message to college students and others in education who can make a difference in the life of a child, or go on to help create a world of more understanding and cooperation. I only hope that this story, my story, can and will inspire others to know that it is never too late.

1

Forged in Fury

I WAS TIRED of eating dirt and blood. How long had I endured it? How many years of disgust and disappointment were etched upon my father's face every time I lost? How many times had he called me a sissy? All because I didn't have the heart to pummel my cousins. It was different when he would unleash me on a neighborhood kid or another kid I didn't really know. Despite my increasing skills in martial arts, Dad always seemed disturbed by the fact that I didn't want to *prove* anything through my strength. Until the day I snapped. Sick of being told to "Suck it up!" and not being able to cry in the face of my uncle's jeers and my cousins' triumphant faces . . . biting back the tears on bruised and battered lips that had been busted open again and again . . . I usually just took it. Until that day.

The curtains and blinds were drawn as usual at my Uncle Harry's large house in Bell Gardens, where we were having a family gathering. I never understood why they liked to keep the golden California sun out of their immaculate living room. It made everything appear gloomy and smaller than it really was. Coming out of the bathroom, I noticed the huge console television and the dark-colored couches where my cousins Brenda and Patty were talking softly. Uncle Harry had gotten off an exhausting cross-country haul and was in the bedroom with Aunt Rita. A trucker like my dad, I knew the ramifications of waking him, so I tiptoed across the thick shag carpet, preparing to go outside. I could hear my little brothers and the rest of my cousins still playing and Mom talking to some aunts and uncles in the kitchen. It was starting out like a typical family gathering, which would eventually include lots of beer drinking and the inevitable arguments between my dad and his brothers about politics, religion, or who claimed the title of best truck driver in the family.

Suddenly, someone came up behind me and pushed me violently. It took me by surprise, and I immediately got pissed off. I was always on guard outside the house because we were Leyden boys, after all, and expected to work out our issues through our fists. Inside, I thought I was safe, if only for a moment. I had let my guard down. It must be Bobbie or Gilbert or maybe Tony, ready to prove their machismo and continue the pecking order in the family.

Before I turned, I heard a laugh and knew that it was Bobbie. He was seven months younger than me, although we were about the same size. How many times had he struck me down? I didn't know. He always wanted to be the tough guy. I'd given him a good pounding from time to time just to save a little face, but he'd beaten me more times than I cared to admit. I felt something snap within me at the sound of his laugh. He was showing off in front of the girls.

As I whipped around, Bobbie tried to throw a punch at me. A burning rage filled my entire body, but I kept my cool. *Discipline, order, control . . .* my lessons flowed easily in the heat of that moment. I blocked Bobbie's punch, then kicked him a couple of times in the face. He was surprised and became irate as he tried to punch me—once, twice, three times. I'd had enough. Utilizing his forward motion, in one swift and fluid movement, I grabbed his fingers and twisted his entire hand and arm behind him until I heard audible snapping and crunching. Bobbie started screaming loudly. When I finally noticed the girls were screaming too, I let go.

Gilbert, Tony, and Mike ran in from outside while the rest of the house was in an uproar. People came from all directions to find out what the screaming was all about. When Gilbert saw his crumpled little brother, his face turned purple. "I'm going to kick your butt!" he fumed, and pushed me menacingly. I thought I was dead, but I had so much adrenaline, I knew I could do some major damage before I went down—major enough that he might never mess with me again. Shocked at that new thought rolling in my head, I prepared to fight him. Oddly enough, from out of nowhere stepped my dad. I thought he was next door at Grandpa Leyden's house.

"Leave him alone," Dad said authoritatively, and Gilbert backed off.

Revenge was in his eyes, but he knew better than to show disrespect to his elders. I'm pretty sure the blood completely drained from my face, but it had little to do with Gilbert. *Dad? Sticking up for me?*

Mom and Aunt Net began arguing heatedly. Aunt Net was furious with me as she was tending to Bobbie, tears streaming down his face. I almost knew how he felt. I also knew I had crossed a line.

"You shouldn't let him use his karate!" Net shrieked. Her voice reflected the frustration I'd often heard in my mother's voice when things got out of control in any Leyden household.

"Bobbie's been beating the crap out of Tommy for a long time," my mother responded grimly, "and you know it. Obviously Tommy's had enough."

Uncle Bob sidled over to Bobbie and looked at the damage.

"Stop blathering," he told him. "Suck it up." Bobbie quieted down almost immediately, but I could tell he was still in considerable pain. I looked away.

The family party was over. Everyone disbanded as Bobbie was rushed to the doctor. I piled into the Ford with Mat and Phil. It was silent the nearly hour-long drive to Fontana, and my gut was filled with a mixture of elation and fear.

A few hours later, Aunt Net called to give my dad the news. I watched him carefully as my mom and I listened to the conversation.

"Bobbie had to go to the hospital," Net informed my dad. I could hear the cold tone of her voice over the phone. "Tommy broke three of Bobbie's fingers and forced his shoulder right out of the socket—it was completely dislocated. I told you, you shouldn't let him use his karate." Dad turned and looked at me and, for a moment, I couldn't read him. My blood ran cold.

"Tell Bobbie not to fight him anymore," he said smugly, and hung up the phone. He smiled, then walked over and hugged me. "You sure taught him a lesson, son. You should've done it years ago." He tousled my hair, almost lovingly, and walked away. I stared after him. *How long had I waited for that look of pride from my father?*

I couldn't face my mother. Like my father, I avoided her gaze and walked out.

TAKING THE BLAME

As far back as I can remember, I felt responsible for the violence and anger between my parents. It wasn't until much later that I realized their relationship had been twisted from the beginning—coming into marriage fully loaded with issues that had not been resolved in their childhood.

My parents talked about meeting at my father's work, and it was love at first sight. My dad was immediately attracted to my mother, but he admits that along with his attraction came the realization that getting married to her would solve two major problems: he could get out of his house—away from the disturbing alcoholism, abuse, and neglect there— and he could also dodge the draft. He quickly found that he had married a woman suffering from deep, emotional traumas of her own.

My mother, Sharon Lynn Reese, had contracted polio when she was only a year old. She survived but would walk with a limp for the rest of her life. Her mother passed away when she was five, and her once-doting father was distraught over the death and became subsequently unavailable for her and her little brother. Within a short time he married again to provide them with a mother but was so cut off emotionally he couldn't—or wouldn't—grasp the fact that his new wife was an alcoholic and that she took out her violent rages on his children. By the time my mother met my dad, she was ready to get away from home any way she could. My parents married when they were still teenagers, each carrying unresolved emotional baggage.

My folks were already separated at the time I was born in 1966. Despite their volatile relationship, my dad had the strong desire to be a good father, and he talked Mom into bringing me home to him so the three of us could become a family. Phil, then Mat, were born over the next five years. My mom loved being a mother, especially when we were young. She kept an immaculately tidy house and always fed us well. She hated her life as an abused child, and she swore never to do it to her own kids. We meant the world to her, and we also tested her boundaries daily, learning that she was far more lenient with three boys than she ever should have been. In fact, there were always two sets of rules for us to live by: one when my father was at home, and one when he was away.

When Dad was home, there was little conversation at the table, much less rebuttal and debate. It was only "Yes, sir! No, sir!" or "Yes, Ma'am! No, Ma'am!" He didn't want to listen to our opinions, and there was never back talk. Mom's dinner rules meant that if we didn't like something, we could make a sandwich. Dad's dinner rules meant we had to finish everything on our plate, even if we didn't like it. Even if we hated it.

Even if it made us gag. It was a huge double standard because Dad didn't have to follow this rule. I hated peas and lima beans so badly that I could barely stand to look at them, much less try to gag them down. A couple of times I had nearly thrown everything back up.

"You eat that now or you'll get a spanking," he growled at me. I sighed and turned my backside to him. I think that was the last time Mom made lima beans while Dad was home.

My dad stood about five foot nine with a full head of dark hair. Out of all his brothers, he was the only one with a muscular build and broad shoulders. Dad wore his hair oiled and slicked back. He donned a white T-shirt and jeans most of the time. Every once in a great while he'd grow out a mustache with a very fifties appearance, but he generally preferred to be clean-shaven. When the television series *Happy Days* came out, some kids in our neighborhood strode up to Dad, their thumbs out, big grins on their faces.

"Heeeeeeyyyy!" they said. We were laughing. He responded in kind and laughed too, but the kids didn't hang around for very long. No one ever did. Though Dad and Henry Winkler may have looked a lot alike, my dad was a very intimidating man. He had learned a lot from his own father.

We liked going to Grandpa Leyden's house, though honestly it had little to do with him. Our grandmother was very kind and we always knew we were loved when we were in her presence, even if that meant we had to put up with lots of kisses. I didn't mind so much because she told us great stories and she also had the candy drawer from hell. As soon as we walked in, Grandma would lavish us with more sweets and goodies than we would ever got in a year at home. Dad could never say anything, and somehow we kids knew it, too. It was the only time I witnessed my father not being in control. If Grandpa wasn't around, Dad might start to say, "Jesus Christ, Mom, do you have to give them all this sugary crap—" and it would take only seconds for Grandma to come after him with a broom for taking the Lord's name in vain. If my grandfather was there, Dad wouldn't even bother opening his mouth. Just like in our home, rules were different when the man of the house was home.

SEEDS OF INTOLERANCE

Grandpa Leyden was staunch Irish-Catholic: fiery in temper and colorful in language. With a full head of thick, black hair, like my father, he was clean-shaven every day. He spoke fluid Gaelic and always wanted to teach me and my brothers and cousins, but none of us were ever interested. His parents had come over from Ireland so his father could work for the Great Northern Railway Company. While his folks spoke Gaelic to each other, they made my grandfather learn English, no excuses. It was a very authoritative home, and Grandpa grew up with that sort of thinking—black/white, right/wrong—and he seemed determined to *always* be right. Dad actually had a lot of things to say about his father . . . as long as he wasn't around.

"You have it so good," my dad often told us, shaking his head. "You have no idea. We didn't even have a dad. We had a fall-down drunk for a father." His eyes flashed as he relived the pain. "If I was lucky, I got a pair of shoes, two pairs of socks, two shirts, and a pair of pants to last me the whole year—no matter how much I grew. I had to wash every other day just to have clean clothes to wear to school. I couldn't wait for the weather to get warmer so I could go barefoot."

"You had *some* good times," my mother interjected once. He gave her a cold stare.

"Yeah," my dad went on, "every once in while, Dad would dry out and our family would move somewhere, get a new start, and begin to have things that most people take for granted—like a real place to sleep and decent food to eat. Then one day we would come home from school and there would be no furniture in the house. Not even a bed for us kids to sleep in, because Dad hocked it all to buy alcohol. By damn, he was going to have his drink—he didn't give a shit if his family had to go without."

I once asked my father how many times he had moved as a kid. He started to count, then got mad and walked away.

It was tough for me to picture Grandpa Leyden as a heavy, heavy drinker, except for a memory I had when I was really little. He and my grandmother were living with us that year, sleeping in a pull-out bed in the living room. One night he fell down a flight of stairs, into our basement. I remember Dad shaking with rage.

"If you ever drink around my kids again," he bellowed, "I'll throw you out into the street. And don't think I wouldn't do it." I never saw Grandpa drink around us after that. Shortly after that, we moved into a bigger house where they had their own room, but they only stayed for a couple of months, until they got a place of their own and moved out.

Grandpa Leyden never showed much loving emotion, except toward my grandmother. He loved her like she was the Virgin Mary. From my father's frequent dissertations, I was supposed to see a monster who drank like a fish and took everything away from his wife and kids. However, as my grandmother grew older and couldn't walk very well, the man I witnessed would accommodate her every wish and whim. Even on the hottest California day, dressed to the nines in his long-sleeved shirts, he would lovingly push her in her wheelchair wherever she needed to go.

Still, I knew that this thin, wiry man had a much darker side to him. I learned that his long sleeves were meant to cover his tattoos. From bits of conversations—usually picked up when the grown-ups were drinking—I learned that Grandpa had spent some time in prison. A few times when I snuck a peak at him on his way out of the bedroom before he rolled his sleeves down, I saw the poorly inked prison tattoos of a dagger on one arm and a pinup girl on the other. In addition to long sleeves, he always wore a white T-shirt under his Pendleton's, with a medal of the Virgin Mary pinned in the V of the T-shirt near his collar. It was important to him to look presentable.

Presentable or not, if my grandfather had something to say, he would let you know. Apparently that mouth almost got him killed once or twice. As a young man in Minnesota, he tried to join the oldest white suprema- cist group in the United States. He and a friend went to a Ku Klux Klan (KKK) rally one night. The speaker asked if anyone in the crowd was Catholic, expecting a fierce, resounding, "NO!" He was shocked when my grandfather raised his hand. The only reason Grandpa wasn't lynched on the spot was because his friend stood up for him and got him out—quick. The KKK used to hate Catholics almost as badly as they hated blacks. He was lucky to get away with his life, but he kept his racist attitudes.

"Never bring home a darkie, boy," he would tell me, his voice grave and serious. "And if you ever marry someone who is not Catholic, I'll disown you!" Oh, then there was my personal favorite, "If you ever wear orange on St. Patrick's Day, I'll kill you!" Now, there was a man who knew his priorities.

Both my grandparents came from a generation of whites that didn't believe in race mixing. I had to respect what they said because they were my elders—no matter what their beliefs were. So though my parents were not *openly* racist, they tolerated a lot of racist attitudes on both sides of the family. My mother's father, Grandfather Reese, was fairly open, except for his issue with Hispanics. He told me and my brothers once that he didn't ever want us to "bring a beaner home" for a wife. This was interesting because two of his stepdaughters married Hispanics. I came to believe he had his head on straight in other matters, however. Stories that this burly yet gentle man told me eventually came to mean a great deal to me— much, much later in my life when I had tough decisions to make. Unlike my other grandfather, when Grandpa Reese had opinions on things, he usually would only share them with me in private. His wife, who was really my stepgrandmother, was often standoffish and cold toward my family. To add insult to the injuries this alcoholic, abusive woman caused my mom when she was little, my mom's stepmother also spurred a lot of problems between my mom and my dad, and even with my dad's parents. It added to the tension that was present in our home, and it only got worse as we grew older.

My brothers and I got pretty good at reading stress levels between my mom and dad. If they started arguing about something, I would hustle my brothers outside to play, or build tents with them in our rooms and hibernate for a while. I would do anything I could to protect my brothers, but I couldn't protect them from the growing hatred between my parents and the blackness that was beginning to creep into our hearts and souls. We pretended that everything was fine and hoped if we made enough happy noise, the neighbors wouldn't really know what was going on. We hoped beyond hope that our parents would catch on and leave each other alone.

As a trucker, Dad was gone more often than not, so we'd just wait out the storm until he clambered back into his truck and onto the road again. He also couldn't handle living in one place for very long. It may have had something to do with him moving so much as a kid. We never knew when another move was imminent.

"Ah, I don't like living here anymore," Dad would say out of the blue. Then we'd up and move across town—always to another house in the same town. I went to Cyprus, Maple, West Randall, Oleandar, and Poplar elementary schools. It didn't matter if my brothers and I had made the best of friends there. Dad was uncomfortable, and so it was time to go.

One day when I was about eight, shortly after one such move, Dad was home and we were playing around, wrestling and having a blast. He could be so fun when he was in a good mood. He said how much he missed us when he was gone. A couple of new friends stopped by but I told them I couldn't play. I didn't like having friends over when Dad was home. I didn't always know what would happen, or when his mood would change. As we wrestled around, Mat started to tell Dad about a bully that lived in our new neighborhood. He'd been giving me and my brothers a bad time. My antenna sent off a warning signal as Dad's voice changed, getting deeper and progressively louder as he asked more questions. Fun time was over.

No one messed with the Leyden family. Dad likened us to *The Fighting Sullivans*, his favorite movie about a family of five boys that went into the Navy together. If someone took on one Sullivan, they took on the entire family. This is what my dad thought his family should be like. That's why he put it in my hands to handle the situation with the bully.

"You'd better take care of it," he told me, his eyes cold, "or I'll take care of *you*." I knew what that meant. The neighborhood boy was invited over, and I sent him home, crying. Dad cheered. From then on, if Mat or Phil got picked on, it was my job to handle it. If a guy was bigger than me, he would have to take on all three of us, just like *The Fighting Sullivans*.

Most of the time, my mother only grudgingly put up with it. However, about the time I turned ten, there was a kid who was trying to be a real tough guy. He couldn't get me to rise to his bait so he began talking trash about my mother. He was making fun of her looks and her weight and said that I was a mama's boy. When he said something to her face, that settled it.

"Go kick his butt, Tommy!" she said. I proceeded to literally make a fool of him in front of the whole neighborhood. I kicked him in the head several times, and even in the face, and he couldn't touch me. I didn't just do this one for my mom. I did it for me too. I was finding it made me popular in the neighborhood. Or at least no one messed with me. Most days that seemed a hell of a lot more important.

CALIBRATING "NORMAL"

One thing about my dad is that he tried to show his love for us by providing things he never had as a kid. We always had a very nice house to live in, food on the table, and exceptionally nice clothes. Our Christmases were always huge. My friends would come over to compare booty, and while most kids in the neighborhood had two or three presents to open on Christmas morning, my brothers and I each had fifteen, maybe as many as twenty. One Christmas we had new bicycles, motorcycles, and all the gear to go with them. Dad also bought lavish things for my mom, including fine jewelry, and other insanely expensive gifts.

"This is beautiful, Thomas," I remembered her saying, her face tight with effort. "But how are we going to pay bills?" The day after Christmas, the fighting intensified. Dad was gone for months after that, driving extra shifts and working two jobs. Another holiday, another birthday, and the same cycle repeated.

"I like it better when Dad's working a lot," Phil whispered to me one day as we were out in the yard, pretending my parents weren't fighting.

"Shh," I said, not wanting him to be overheard. I didn't tell him that I preferred it that way, too. The fighting between my parents was becoming almost unbearable. While they had always taken pains not to fight in front of us, most of the time we could hear screaming and name calling through whatever doors they had gone behind. That day was worse. We could hear the sickening sounds of slamming and glass shattering. Things had always been bad at home, but now I was living with a knot in my stomach that never seemed to go away.

One night shortly after I had turned eleven, my dad went out to a bar. He arrived home sloppy drunk, barely making it into the driveway before he passed out. I looked out the window to see Mom trying to pull him out of the car and into the house. He wouldn't go.

"I can't just leave you out here, you idiot," she cried, tugging on him. That's when I saw my father slam her up against the car, hard. I screamed as she crumpled to the ground, and I yelled for Dad to stop. When he heard my voice, he looked up at me in the window. Guiltily, he bent down and tried to help Mom up. She didn't see me but began slapping him and yelling at him in anger for what he'd done. This time I yelled at her to stop; I was screaming and yelling as if all of our lives depended on it. It felt like it did. The neighbors turned on their lights and began coming outside to see what was going on. Embarrassed, my parents hurriedly helped each other into the house and locked the door.

I looked in on Mat and Phil before I went to bed and covered my head with my pillows, just like they were doing.

As things got more heated and out of control at home, I hated my life. I especially hated having to pretend that everything was fine. Our family would go to church and to ball games and picnics and parties and act like everything was just dandy. It was a lie. It sucked.

For the last several months, I was attending Oleander Elementary School. The first and second toughest kids in the whole school were my best friends, John and Joey. I probably could have beaten them both up if I had wanted to, but it was more important for me to be their friends. They were awesome guys. Joey was Hispanic and lots of fun. I also had a crush on his little sister. She was very, very pretty—petite with large, dark eyes and dark brown hair.

One Sunday I went with my family to church at St. Mary's, across from Fontana Junior High. I was hoping to see Joey's sister. The church was beautiful inside, yet it always creeped me out. It was so very silent, like walking into a library, except it had stricter rules and mysterious ties to heaven and hell. I tiptoed in, blessing myself with the holy water. I walked down the aisle with my family and found a pew. Kneeling, the boys and I pretended to pray before taking our seats. As I sat there, I remembered when I was small and the whole mass was said in Latin. I had no idea what they were saying, except that I picked up on the words to kneel and stand. I liked it being in English so I could follow along, but my Grandfather Leyden said he would never go to church again. It was interesting to me what seemed to set people off. My parents didn't really care about the change from Latin, but my dad freaked out the first time he saw a Christmas tree in the church. He proclaimed it was blasphemous, and we heard about it for months afterward.

As a young child, I had gone to Catechism every Saturday and church every Sunday. As Catholics, this is what we did. As I got older, however, we started going less and less. I had received my First Communion and I would be getting confirmed soon, but my brothers hardly ever went, and they didn't have to go to Catechism. This Sunday, my parents wanted to go because things were horrible between them again. Church had become a convenience, something they used when things were really bad. I was looking at my family, and I remember being so confused. Here we were at church, the perfect family, dressed and pressed in our Sunday best, participating in Communion as if everything was hunky dory. How many times had I heard my father say, "Don't air your problems outside the home. Don't show your dirty laundry to the world"? I had always thought our living hell was normal. I looked up at the crucifix hanging on the wall. Didn't everybody live that way?

We were early, and I watched several old ladies saying their rosaries. *Hail Mary, full of grace, the Lord is with thee . . .* I shuddered involuntarily. One of my worst beatings happened over that prayer. Of course, my cousin Bobbie and I got a little creative and changed it up for good measure.

"Hail, Mary, full of *grease* . . ." We laughed and laughed, not knowing that my dad had overheard us. He came in and grabbed me.

"You're going to get a good one," he said. I knew what a "good one" meant, but I wasn't prepared for what happened next. He literally had his belt off in less than three seconds, whaling away at me. He whipped my back, my hands, the back of my legs . . . I don't think he stopped for several minutes. The only thing that got me through was knowing that I was not alone, that Bobbie was next. We would commiserate together.

Nothing, however, happened to Bobbie. Aunt Annette laughed it off. I was beaten to a pulp and couldn't sit down for days, and Bobbie simply walked away.

"Never make fun of a prayer again," my dad threatened. I didn't. But now I wondered, if things were so black and white, why Bobbie got off and I got beat. Why my friends didn't have to fight neighborhood bullies. Why some people seemed to have happy homes. Then I realized it was probably all my fault. All the naughty and mean things I'd done had cursed my family.

Every time I went to church, I always knew I was going to hell. Hell to me meant burning alive, always in pain, being constantly stabbed with a pitchfork. When I was a little kid, I accidentally stuck myself with a kitchen fork, and it went deep into my flesh. It hurt badly and it frightened me beyond belief—it actually made me paranoid. Every time I made a mistake at home I heard, "You're going to hell for that!" In my terror, I would go and tell the priest, "I lied about taking an extra soda. I hit my brother Mat with my GI Joe. I did this . . . and I did that . . ." I got the "Our Fathers" and "Hail Marys" down so fast, I could pack several of them into a minute. My penitence became even more streamlined as time went on because I was always doing more things leading me away from the pearly gates. But that day I wondered . . . whose version of the pearly gates would win out? Different people seemed to have different ideas about heaven, just like they did about what normal was. The term *dysfunctional* didn't have any meaning for me yet, but intrinsically I knew that something seemed off, not quite normal within my family.

That was the last time we went to church for quite a while. My parents separated again, and from day to day, I wasn't sure what was going to happen next.

2

Playing the Pawn

I WAS STRONG and active in many sports and was especially good at baseball. My team was the Cardinals. When I was only ten years old, my coach had told me, "You have a lot of talent at this game, TJ. Keep this up and you can really go somewhere with it." He said I had the strength, speed, and skill, but to me the best part was that I loved the game. I started seeing myself playing through junior high and high school, and I even had the shyest dream of someday maybe going on to being a major league player. When I played ball, I felt like I was somebody. I almost felt that knot in the pit of my stomach disappear for a while.

Fontana was a fairly small, tight-knit community. Ball games meant huge family gatherings, and the park would be packed with nearly a hundred people watching—parents, grandparents, neighbors, and friends.

The last game of the season was especially popular. My mom and brothers came to see me play. No one knew where Dad was. The game was going well, and I was playing in the right outfield position. I was feeling high and tight, right on my game. Suddenly there was a huge commotion in the stands. From my position in right field, it was hard for me to tell what was going on. The sick feeling in my stomach came back as I recognized my dad throwing some kind of fit in the stands. I could tell he'd had a little too much to drink. Worse, arm-in-arm with him was his new girlfriend—a bleached-blonde bimbo with half a brain and double the body to boot. Dad told me later he just wanted me to meet her, but I knew he was flaunting her in front of my mother. Mom knew it too, and she was infuriated. She didn't hold back.

I saw the altercation beginning to take place, but I couldn't leave my position and run in. I was distracted from the game. By the time my team got the third out, everything had exploded. Mom had told Dad to leave, and his girlfriend got in on the argument. My mother pushed her, then Dad pushed my mother, and it got so ugly that some other parents got involved and it ended in fist fighting. I couldn't believe my parents were acting this way.

"Get out of here!" several of the people in charge yelled at my dad, who was obviously being belligerent.

"You're just a bunch of coaches!" sneered my dad. "You can't tell me to leave!"

"I can," said the league manager. "What do you think you're doing in front of the kids? You have no right to do this. Now get out of here—and don't you come back for the rest of the season. You are hereby 86'd from this ballpark—got that? You're through here. Now leave."

Dad yelled at him for a few more minutes, then flipped him off on the way out of the stands. If that wasn't bad enough, he came down to see me in the dugout.

"You're coming with me, Tommy," he said. All the players stared at him. My coach glared at my dad, and I noticed he was watching me carefully, ready to step in if necessary.

"No, I'm not." I stood my ground. I wanted him to get the hell out of there and I wanted to go back to playing my game. And I wanted to wipe the entire night from my mind. I was just glad it was the end of the season. He glared back at my coach and then left.

I hoped I could go back to playing the rest of the game—to get my mind off the nasty scene, and to find myself in the game, if just once more. Unfortunately, my mother was so embarrassed that now *she* wanted to leave. She came down into the dugout and this time I had to go. It was humiliating, because now everyone in the ballpark knew who the poor kid with the screwed up parents was, and believe me, they were *all* looking. I will never forget that walk of shame.

Later on that night, Dad showed up at our house.

"Tommy, you're coming with me and you're coming with me NOW." I looked at him like he was nuts.

"I hate you!" I said. "I'm *never* coming with you!" That was the first time I ever told anyone that I hated them. I meant it. I was sick of playing the pawn in this twisted, demented game.

Crazy as it was, my parents got back together a few days after the ball game. Dad moved home again, just in time for our baseball awards banquet and barbecue. We all went as a family and again acted like nothing had happened, that we were the ideal little family. The rest was simply . . . that "dirty laundry" that I wasn't supposed to talk about. I sure wished it wasn't flapping out on the line for the whole world to see.

I know it was probably awkward for everyone there. I'm not sure anyone felt as out of place as I did. As soon as the players received their trophies we left the barbecue. I hated the whispers that followed us back to the car. Whether real or imagined, I hated what those whispers stood for.

From that day forward, I never played the game of baseball with all my heart and soul again. Eventually I also walked away from a brown belt in karate and every other sport and positive activity I was involved in. The world had become an incredibly unfair, shitty place to live.

For several months, I withdrew from everyone, and then I became a split personality. It was easy—after all, I had grown up with the best examples of it. At home, at school, and at church, in front of any authority figures, I was a fine, upstanding citizen. On my own, I began living a totally different life. At Oleander Elementary, I was respectful to my teacher, but I didn't do any of my homework. I was socializing, hanging out, and having make-out sessions with the girls. I was a chameleon. I changed my colors to get along with others. I had friends of all different backgrounds, races, religions, and creeds because I could easily change who I was, just to fit in. Just to belong somewhere. I began to try things I had never done before—things I wouldn't have even considered doing before.

When my mom found out about my homework issue, she developed a new plan. As a teacher's aide at Poplar Elementary, she made me transfer from Oleander so she could keep an eye on me. The only thing was, I wasn't doing homework there, either. One day, the vice principal illustrated exactly why it was important to complete homework at that school. In front of my mother, he struck me with a wooden cutting board paddle. It was not a soft landing. In fact, it made me cry. I was trying to be tough, and I hoped my mother wouldn't tell my father as tears escaped my clenched eyes. Now aware of the consequences, I decided I had better get my homework done, and I got good grades for the rest of the year. Grades only counted for a portion of my life, however. By the time I was twelve years old, in 1978, I had started drinking, had my first sexual experience, and had started doing drugs. I had been in lots of fights—many spurred on by my own father. I began to feel a raw hatred so strong it encompassed every part of my life. I felt like the world was my enemy.

Within a few years, I would even be at war.

The next year I started school at Fontana Junior High. I lived in the Alder school district, but my parents didn't want me going there because of the "influences" there. Alder had very few whites, and Fontana Junior High was almost all white. Instead of going to the school a few blocks away, I had to ride my bike five miles to school and then five miles back every day. I didn't feel sorry for myself because this was, after all, California. I also had a four-hundred-dollar tricked-out BMX custom-built bike my father had given me, and I loved riding it and doing wheelies. I loved the time away from everything and everyone. I felt free.

The good news about moving so often is that I had established a reputation in every school I'd lived in. So when I went to Fontana Junior High for the first time, people from Cyprus, Maple, West Randall, Oleandar, and Poplar elementary schools all knew me—or at least knew of my reputation. Because of that reputation, I only had to fight twice my entire junior high career.

One day, some kid was really, really getting on my nerves. I chased the guy down several times all over the quad, in between fist-fighting. He would throw wild punches and then run away, but I didn't let up until he was a bloody mess. All the kids kept cheering and yelling until we were pulled apart by two teachers and taken to see Mr. Rossey, the vice principal. A massive ex-Marine, he meant business. He asked who the aggressor was, and I admitted it was me. He let the other student get cleaned up and go back to class, then proceeded to call my parents, letting them know the situation and that I was about to get paddled. Mr. Rossey had a special paddle with holes in it for aerodynamic capability. He only hit me twice, but it literally lifted me off my feet and made it difficult to sit for a week. That was the most trouble I got in that day, because Dad only asked me if I won or not.

That was the year I began hanging out with a lot of party kids and a lot more of the tougher kids in the crowd. Kids would bring alcohol from their homes, or we would have someone buy it for us. We mixed it and drank it right on the school premises. For whatever reason, we thought that was so cool. Later on, others started to bring a little coke to school, or a little weed before class. We hung out at Miller Park, known affectionately as Stoner Park. Most of my friends were upper-middle class white kids. A lot of the girls were either very pristine, "good" girls or very loose girls. It didn't matter. We all hung out together.

Josephine Zorrelli, my English teacher, was the only reason I survived the curriculum of junior high. She's the one who inspired me to read all sorts of books, which I learned that I actually loved to do. Suffering from dyslexia since I was young, I always felt rather stupid, even when teachers told me I was brilliant. Zorrelli introduced me to new books and classics like *Where the Red Fern Grows*. For myself and other guys who struggled with spelling, she would hold Saturday classes on her own time. We actually came. (It didn't hurt that Mrs. Zorrelli was really good looking, and that she was the aunt of my friend Albert Steven Scofanni, who called himself "ASS.") By the time I was in eighth grade, I could read like crazy, loved it, and could pass spelling tests.

I felt bad for disappointing Mrs. Zorrelli when two other kids and I were caught blowing toilets off the wall with M-80s. We made another exciting trip to Mr. Rossey's office to receive another paddling and expulsion. This time, we knew it was coming and we all wore jeans. It only took two days to be able to sit down.

INFANTILE MADNESS

That year my mom and dad had once again decided to call it quits. They said this time it was for good. They started divorce proceedings and then carried on like children. They were both depressed and suicidal. Then they went out and bought fancy cars, fancy clothes, and almost always ended up in the same clubs, particularly the Branding Iron and the Fontana Inn. I'm almost convinced they did it on purpose.

Not long after, my dad came home after a night out on the town. He had bloody scratches and deep gouges across his face.

"Your crazy mom got into it again," he said, as if that explained it all. "She gets these jealous rages, and I don't know what to do with her."

Mom arrived home shortly thereafter, and she was extremely emotional. We ran into our rooms, but I overheard her yelling at him, saying that she was sick of all the head games he was constantly playing with her.

"You say you love me," she raged, "but then you go off dancing and drinking with other women, like that woman tonight. You were trying to get her to go home with you! Why do you keep doing that? Why do you want to tear my heart out like that?"

Another night, my mom saw my father leaving one of the clubs and waving to some woman from his brand-new, itty-bitty Porsche. She revved up her car and proceeded to slam her brand-new Z28 Camaro into his Porsche and then drove off. Dad came home in a rage and was going to have her arrested. The boys and I protested.

"You can't put Mom in jail!" we wailed, pleading with him.

"She's acting like a flipping lunatic!" he ranted.

You both are lunatics, I thought. *Teenage freaking lunatics. Even my friends don't act this way.*

Things like this were happening almost every week between my parents. I stalked off to my room and shut the door. The crazier behavior the boys and I witnessed, the more Mat wanted to comfort Dad, the more Phil wanted to comfort Mom, and the more I just wanted to get away. I was finding all kinds of ways to get away.

3

SETTING THE STAGE FOR RAGE

BY THE TIME I was thirteen, I had walked away from all of my positive identifiers like sports and most academics. In having friends from all backgrounds, I got a taste of much of what the world had to offer. I especially enjoyed music. I think I listened to every kind of music known to mankind. As soon as I heard punk rock, however, I was sucked right in. It set the stage for my violence.

Punk rock music and the venues it was played at spoke to me in a language I understood—the fear, rage, and chaos that was so familiar. Only this time, *I* was the one who was in control; *I* had the power. I was the one yelling, and I didn't care who was yelling back. When there was real violence, I was the one perpetrating it. I loved the beat, the head games, the cruel aggression in the mosh pits, the crowd surfing, the stage diving. It was pure, raw power, and I craved it. Sweat and adrenaline—I was addicted.

At first I was simply a punk rock kid. I made deliberate holes in my jeans, wore chains around my biker boots, and had my hair all spiked up. One day I got my head shaved into a Mohawk. I wore it for a day, and it was cool, but it wasn't me. The next day I shaved it all off. It's funny, but when I shaved my head, it felt "right" to me. It was clean, it was mean—it looked perfect. I stopped wearing the Pendleton's and started wearing preppy shirts and wife beaters (white tank tops). I looked in the mirror and realized I *looked* like a bad-ass Skinhead. I even felt like one. I wondered if all the Skinheads I had seen in the pits at the concerts felt the same way.

At home I begged my mom to get me a pair of Doc Marten boots, but I couldn't wait. I borrowed some from other people so I could look the part until she was tired of the whining and caved. She thought it was just a phase I was going through. My new pair of Doc Martens were oxblood red. I bought a green M-1 Bomber flight jacket. That's what the Skins wore. Some of my closest friends started digging the same music and scene as I was, and I encouraged them to buy the boots, shirts, jackets, and oxblood red braces when they could afford it. Dad gave me piles of money all the time, so when my friends couldn't afford some of the clothing, I would let them borrow some of my mine or give them clothing. That way, we all had the look together and fit right in at the concerts.

The best concert venues were in Hollywood and Los Angeles. We hung out at Madame Wong's (godmother of punk), Whiskey a Go-Go's, and dive places in Hollywood. We went to bigger gatherings at the Palladium, the El Ray Theatre, and the Olympic Auditorium, which had more room to thrash fellow attendees while dancing. The first bands I got into were *The Germs, Bad Brains, Circle Jerks,* and *Black Flag.* As other bands came on the scene, I began to shift. I particularly enjoyed the really hard-core metallic bands—*Ozzy Osbourne, Iron Maiden, Judas Priest,* and any other sound with an angry, addictive beat.

Mosh pits were the most compelling to me—bloody, negative energy in all its glory. I threw myself into the pits with every ounce of adrenaline and fury I had. I loved the pushing and the shoving. I didn't care if I got hurt. I didn't care if someone else got hurt. I was there to vent my rage all over everybody. I think I punched at least one person in the face during every concert I went to. My cousin Gilbert thought I was nuts for going to these events.

"You don't want to go to those shows, man," Gilbert said. "You've got to be wacked! You're crazy."

I just laughed. I *was* crazy—though a smart kind of crazy. I had learned very quickly that music is the most powerful influence in the world. *The* most powerful. It could cross cultural lines, spiritual lines, and bring all different kinds of messages. It brought me the message I wanted. I believed it was acceptable to be filled with hate. I believed it was acceptable to be violent. More important, I felt *accepted.*

POWER AND POLITICS

During concerts, people started to watch me, to notice me. The savvy ones wanted to harness the power they saw in me for their own ends.

Skins in particular wouldn't bump into me like they had at first; they gave me a nod as they passed. I was watching them closely as well. I enjoyed studying the groups that monitored the mosh pits. They controlled how the concerts went, including *when* and *if* it got ugly, as well as against *whom*. In the mosh pit, Skins would stand shoulder-to-shoulder in the middle section and control the pit by pushing people around, in a crowd control sort of way. They were hostile in a friendly manner. However, if a Skin was the victim of something other than pleasant moshing, I watched the consequences with interest. Once the Skin pointed at the guy, the line in the middle would dissolve as they surrounded him and beat him down.

Concert goers were not the only victims. If bands made ugly remarks about Skins, I saw them literally pulled offstage and beaten until the bouncers could get the crowd under control. Everyone got out of the way for the Skins, because if they didn't, they would soon be dead, or close to it. Whether you liked them or not, you had to deal with them, and you'd better be nice.

I wanted to have that kind of authority and command. I particularly paid attention to a group called Circle One—the real players, in my book. I listened and learned avidly. It was not surprising that they happened to be the group of Skins that showed the most interest in me as well.

One night at age fourteen, I was attending a concert at the Olympic Auditorium in downtown LA, a huge place where they hold boxing matches. I had been drinking and took a break during the concert to use the bathroom. A massive Skinhead stepped out of the shadows and stopped me, his arms barring the doorway. He didn't seem to want to fight me, so I listened to what he had to say.

"You do *not* want to go in there right now," he said.

I needed to go! I almost felt like fighting him, but the look in his eye and the feeling it gave me stopped me cold. The hair on the back of my neck prickled ominously, and I decided to stay outside. The Skin then relaxed and actually joked with me for half a minute before we heard fists slamming, kicking, and then screaming from inside the bathroom. After several long minutes, some guys came out, smirking. I went in, and some poor idiot lay in a bloody pulp on the floor, barely alive. I stepped over him and did my thing. On my way out, I stopped to thank the Skin for warning me about the fight. That could have been hell. We had a beer together and laughed over the whole thing. One thing was for certain,

I didn't want to be the poor idiot in the bathroom. I'd had enough of that crap in my lifetime. In my mind I had twisted life to the point that there was only predator and prey, and I knew what end of the gun I wanted to be holding.

I soon became friends with all the Skins from Circle One. They operated in South Bay and Torrance, fully two hours of freeway driving away—far enough from home that it wasn't convenient to hang out on an everyday basis. I only saw them at shows. When an event was over, I had to drive the opposite direction to go home. Still, their influence on me was profound. These gang members, all four to six years older than I, treated me like I was one of their own. Of course I listened to their advice! They told me about a local group of Skins in my neighborhood, and I decided to hook up with them. I had no idea at the time what consequences this choice would bring to my life.

Since things were still outrageously out of control at home, at first I got fed up, and then I got smart. I decided to play both sides to see what I could get out of this mess called my family. It worked beautifully. My parents hated each other so much they wouldn't talk to one another—for *any* reason. I could tell my mom I was staying at my dad's, and she would never call there to check on me, and vice-versa. For the first time in my life outside of a mosh pit, I felt powerful and free.

By the time I turned fifteen, this sport had gotten really good for me. My dad, in his attempts to reach me (and really piss off my mom), bought me a car. It was a '66 Pontiac LeMans with a 326—the muscle car that looked like a GTO. It was my baby, and she was cocoa brown with gold flakes and an awesome tan interior. It didn't matter that I didn't have a license yet. When I showed the car to my mom, she was infuriated with my father. Still, she turned around and bought me a killer car stereo. Of course, as soon as I showed my dad my new stereo, he bought me new tires and rims. It was all playing out wonderfully, and I felt like life was finally giving me what *I* wanted. I had become better at manipulating my parents, my friends, and even my teachers. I was learning power.

I had been AWOL from home a lot before, but with a car, home life was history. It was easy to find someone to sneak out with at night and go cruising around with them. My friends thought my car was awesome, and there was lot of power in having it. I had more friends; I had access to alcohol and to lots of girls. In addition, any time a girl was upset with her parents or just wanted to run away for a couple of days, she would call me. We would go to the park, hang out, talk, drink, and whatever else she would do. Then I usually ended up taking her home.

The year I turned sixteen, my parents finally got divorced after bouncing back and forth for three years. When the divorce was finalized, the boys and I felt the whole gamut of emotions reflective of the emotional roller coaster we had been on. I had experienced a few times of joy when it seemed like my family was strong and we would make it. Most of the time, however, the tension and violence had been so horrible and awkward for so long that something inside of us felt jubilant! We knew it should have happened years ago.

At least that's how I felt because I honestly believed my brothers and I might have some peace now. No one was prepared for what happened next—especially me. My parents became more suicidal, especially my dad. And now instead of playing the psychological games of death and guilt with my mom, he did it to me and my brothers, and it seemed like he meant it.

One night we were having a bit of party. The boys and I all had friends over, and Dad and Uncle Harry were drinking. I'm not really sure what exactly was going on in my dad's life that brought him to that point that night, but looking back, it was a terrible joke. We had a house full of people and yet he locked himself in the only bathroom and swallowed twenty or so sleeping pills. Like no one was going to find him!

I kicked in the door, and my dad was sitting on the floor, the empty bottle of sleeping pills on the sink. Someone called 911.

"What the hell are you doing, knucklehead?" screamed my Uncle Harry. Dad wouldn't answer.

One of my friends, my uncle, and I picked him up and took him to his room. By the time we made it to the bed, the paramedics were already knocking on the door. They came in and talked to my dad and took the empty pill bottle from me as they asked him questions. He refused treatment.

"Get the hell out of here!" Dad said.

"Okay," the paramedics replied, shrugging, and they simply backed up to the door of the bedroom, arms folded, waiting.

"What are you doing?" he cried out, enraged.

"Oh, we're just standing here until you pass out." One of them glanced at his watch. Within seconds, Dad's eyes rolled into the back of his head, and he fell backward. BOOM. The paramedics had him laid out on the ground. One was taking his vital signs while the other shoved a tube down his throat, pushing dark, chocolate-looking charcoal into his stomach to soak up the poison.

"He's going to blow chunks!" they warned us, and we backed away.

A minute later as they were wheeling him to the door, Dad woke up and vomited violently. The paramedics tried to catch the contents in the bag to make sure they knew everything he had downed in the attempt to off himself. As they put him in the ambulance and I watched them drive away, I was terrified for my father's life. And deep within me, my innermost, secret worry was that he would die because I hadn't stopped him in time and *I* would be blamed for it.

Anytime I was either at Dad's or Mom's, it seemed like the drama was continually building. I felt ready to explode at any minute, and I would take those feelings outside, into concerts, into fights, and vent that rage somewhere else. Someone had to have a cool head for Mat and Phil's sake, and it certainly wasn't either of my parents. Shortly after my father's attempted suicide, my mother started bringing boyfriends over to spend the night. I was furious and resentful toward her, though truthfully, she wasn't doing anything my father hadn't done to our family all our lives. (We found out later that I had a half brother born in 1967, ten months after me, conceived with one of my dad's old girlfriends. I would not meet Eric until he and I were about thirty-five years old.) My little brothers had each picked a parent to cling to; it was easier that way. I was right in the middle, pulled relentlessly on both sides. I was the trump card, and it seemed as if they each felt they would have more power in the situation if I was on their side. I was sick of it.

School became the least of my priorities, and I stopped going that year. At least, I quit going to learn. On a typical day I would drive to the school parking lot, where I would pick up a bunch of friends and go cruising for a while. We'd come back at lunch and I would split with more friends to get some booze for our afternoon and evening adventures.

If we were feeling wealthy, we'd have any number of beverages at our disposal. If we were poor that day, someone would buy a bottle of Thunderbird for a cheap (and nasty) thrill. My biggest love was alcohol, and I drank every day. I had fake IDs, I had money, and I had friends with money that would buy some for me because I always had the car. My addiction to alcohol happened very quickly. I couldn't just drink a beer or two. I had to have a beer or two every fifteen minutes. Every once in a while, I'd wake up with a really bad hangover, then I'd go have two or three beers, and I'd be okay for the rest of the day. As soon as I was feeling better, however, I was throwing back the drinks again.

Sometimes I drove over to Fontana Junior High to pick up some girls. I'd always check the mailbox at my two homes, especially around report card time. Then I would drop everyone off at their homes and I might go to Mom's for dinner, or to get money from my dad. Gas was cheap at only seventy-five to eighty-five cents a gallon, and I would cruise around with my friends and girlfriends until the wee hours of the morning. I have no idea how many miles I put on that car. No one messed with us because we looked and acted the part of intimidating Skinheads. The next day would start all over again, back at the parking lot at school.

Every once in a while, I ran into a teacher that had somehow had a rare opportunity to get to know me before I totally quit school. I was always prepared for a look of disgust, but I was surprised by one who had a tear in her eye.

"You're much too brilliant to quit like this, TJ," she said. "You have too much potential. You don't have to throw your life away."

THE ILLUSION OF HAVING IT ALL

I didn't feel like I was throwing anything away, or missing out on a single aspect of life. After all, I had a car, I had girls, I had booze, a reputation as a bad-ass, and a nightlife that most kids my age or even older would kill for. By the time I turned sixteen, I had gotten my first tattoo, I had extremely close friends, and my mom and my brothers had moved to a nice place in Redlands. My mom never knew that I was failing school because I was the one who was home to get the mail and erase the answering machine. I had it good. *Wasn't that what life was all about? Getting what you wanted?*

In the meantime, I hit as many punk rock and heavy metal concerts as I could. This was the time that I really began to become entrenched into the Skinhead Movement.

I loved being a Skin. It was all about venting my rage, partying, and having a good time. It was the perfect lifestyle for me and filled all my needs. It filled a lot of white teenagers' needs, especially boys. All the men in my family were truckers or worked hard out on the docks. They worked hard and played hard—and playing hard meant they would go out after their shifts to clubs and drink. We weren't much different from the fathers in the homes we grew up in. We drank as much as we weighed, we partied hard, and we worked hard the next day. Because of this, the Skinhead

Movement attracted a lot of kids at first. It was grass roots America. Especially since the punk scene had coke and heroine floating around, we knew we weren't about that. The punk kids kind of went hippy (except that their hair was pink and green), and they thought we were conservative. As punks became more anti-American, Skinheads became more nationalist. Ronald Reagan was president, and there was a lot of "Love America or Leave It" sentiment in the air. The Skinhead philosophy at that time was very, very simple. We all had American flags on our jackets. We defended America to the hilt, going overboard on occasion, and we didn't care.

At a concert we saw a punk kid with an anarchy symbol—just a symbol—on his jacket.

"Do you know what this symbol is?" I asked him. "Do you know what it stands for?"

"Anarchy," he said proudly.

"You want anarchy?" I snarled at him. "I'll give you anarchy."

We began punching and hitting him until he was down on the ground.

"You should love America! It's America that has laws and rules against beating the crap out of you like this. You want anarchy, I'll give it to you. I've got the power. I think you should love America." And we gave him one last kick in the symbol for good measure. Then we laughed and walked away, arm in arm, as people backed away from us every time they saw us coming.

Skins were my family, the people who looked out for me, the people who were loyal and stuck up for me and would even fight for me. I wasn't about to go anywhere else, do anything else, be anything else but a Skin. Still, I wasn't quite prepared for the SHARPs. In fact, the whole state of California was unprepared for this alternate Skinhead gang who came in and set the stage for violent, racist factions . . . and for rage.

4

RAPID ESCALATION

AS I DELVED further into the Skinhead culture, I discovered more and more about the politics of the group. It's interesting that I had become fully entrenched just as international events were about to shape who Skins were and what we stood for.

Skinheads in America—especially in Southern California—stood simply for violence. We loved ourselves, we loved America, and we definitely loved the party scene. It was all about presentation and intimidation. In our Doc Martens, slim suspenders, button-down shirts, bomber jackets, and shaved heads, we looked like bad-asses and people showed us respect out of fear. We weren't racist or Nazi extremists like some of our brothers in Europe. At that time, Skins in California were all brothers, including many, many Hispanics and even a few blacks! *Race did not matter then*. As long as you were mean and strong and patriotic, as long as you were a Skin, you were *it*.

Before long, however, the SHARPs factionalized what it meant to be a Skinhead. They were Skin Heads Against Racial Prejudice. It might have sounded like a pretty cool thing to be involved in to some punk kids, and a lot of people joined their ranks. But the international movement of SHARPs—which had come from Europe into New York and had found its way to California—was severely twisted. The first time I met some SHARPs, we were partying in a mosh pit. They came up to one of my buddies at a concert, where the music was loud and the adrenaline was high and focused.

"Hey, man," one SHARP said. "Doesn't it piss you off when a black man takes your woman?" Well of course it pissed him off. It would piss him off if it was a white man or Hispanic man—he would have been ticked at any man that took his girl.

"Yeah, man, that pisses me off," he agreed. They proceeded to beat the crap out of him for being a racist. We were furious. We didn't let them get away with that. Now we were targeted as racist Skins—so far from the truth it was pitiful.

Still, we began watching this group carefully. They were causing factions all around us. They approached another friend of ours in the pit one night, and we weren't anywhere around to do something about it.

"Hey, dude, are you white pride?"

"Yeah!" he replied. He was proud of being American, proud of being white, proud of listening to awesome music. He would've been proud of anything at that moment. His answer to white pride wasn't about being racist—it was about being happy to be white in that moment. To us, the original Skins, many blacks and Hispanics were our brothers.

The SHARPs ganged up on him and beat the shit out of him.

"Freakin' Nazi!" they screamed. "Who do you think you are, being white pride?"

If the SHARPs hadn't come along in our group, I believe rival factions would not have evolved as quickly or to the extent that they did. We would have all just been having a good time partying. The SHARPs forced us to pick. Kids were getting beat up and thrown in jail, and it wasn't a game anymore. We *had* to pick. We all lived in upper-middle class neighborhoods that were 95 percent white, and so part of it was a no-brainer. The SHARPs stood for something so bizarre and outrageous (plus they had pissed us off), we began to hate them and everything they stood for. Apparently, however, it was happening from both sides.

Which came first, the chicken or the egg? The SHARPs definitely pushed me and my boys into being neo-Nazi Skinheads. For others, however, it was the Nazis pushing them into becoming SHARPs, beating them up for not being white pride. Who caused the chasm first? I don't know. But since the sides were battling, once you picked a side, you were automatically at war against the other side.

The SHARPs called us boneheads. "You have no brains," they said. "Just bones."

The SHARPs logo had a figure that looked like a Trojan, so we called them Trojan Skins, fake Skins, not real Skins.

"It's kind of like wearing a condom," we'd say. "You go through the motions, but it just doesn't feel the same way." We would pick a fight with them any way we could. We would hunt them down. And we had to watch, because they were hunting us down as well.

In having to choose a more extreme viewpoint and look, we very quickly dropped the traditional look of the red Doc Martens and green flight jackets—especially because that's what the SHARPs wore. We adopted a more militant look, with jet-black Doc Martens, black flight jackets, and black Dickies instead of blue or gray. Our new look aligned more rigidly with our Nazi brothers in Europe. We actually loved it because the black made us look a whole lot more sinister. In addition, we started wearing tan or red shirts. Tan stood for the brown of Nazi SS uniforms, and red stood for the swastika flag. We wore white braces at first, until we developed other color codes to represent acts of violence. In addition, no self-respecting Skin would leave home without his or her Doc Martens, steel-toed for more force when we were kicking the crap out of somebody.

As smart, middle-class white kids, we knew exactly how to play ourselves off as upstanding citizens. To most adults, we looked like honorable and "respectable" white kids. After all, we often kept our tattoos covered, and in our sharp, preppy shirts, clean-cut hair and shiny boots, how could we be capable of anything terrible? Many parents were actually grateful when their kids started cutting their long hair, taking showers, and looking respectable.

We were respectable all right. We dressed so that those who knew us had better respect our power and authority. My friends and I all had shaved heads, or the "number one crop" as Skinheads call it (number one for the attachment size on a barber's cutting clippers). We wore braces or suspenders on our black Dickies or Levis. Everything about our look held meaning. If our suspenders were down, we were looking for a fight. Worn up, everything was cool. If we were taking a girl out, we wore a button-down shirt like a Fred Perry Polo, or better yet a Sherman. Ben Sherman shirts were so hot, people tried to buy them off my back. During casual occasions, we wore wife beaters or black sweatshirts, but always with our Doc Marten boots—and unless it was 100 degrees, our flight jackets. Eventually, some of us would add a confederate flag that hung from shoulder to shoulder on our jackets.

While the SHARPs wore many of the same clothing, their Doc Martens had only eight eyelets. Ours had fourteen eyelets, to stand for "the fourteen words": "We must secure the existence of our people and a future for White children."

The girls in the group had fourteen words too, although it was different from ours: "Because the beauty of the white Aryan woman must not perish from the Earth."

It was not uncommon for people to check out the number of eyelets on my boots so they would know whether to hang out with me, attempt to beat me up, or stay the hell away. They also looked at the color of laces. Prospects wore black until they were jumped in. Then they wore white laces. They could wear red laces after they had committed a violent crime. There were also yellow laces, which stood for anarchy and sometimes stood for assaulting a police officer. At one time or another, my friends and I eventually wore them all. Later it became popular to wear swastika soles screwed into the boots to imprint the hate symbol while beating people up. We cracked up when Screwdriver came out with the song, "If There's a Riot," with these lyrics:

Walking down the street, avoiding the cops
With size ten boots, and a number one crop
People avoid you as you pass by
Only the smart ones know the media lies

Hey, that's us, we thought. *Size ten boots, number one crop. We're the Bootboys.* Bootboy was another name for Skinhead. A boot party was one where we were going to commit a violent assault. We had plenty of boot parties. More than I can count.

It didn't take long to develop racist attitudes and incorporate it all the way. Overnight, being a Skinhead meant that you hated everyone who wasn't white. It was in this warped and twisted way that Skinheads began to align themselves with the philosophy of the White Power Movement. The songs, the attitudes, the propaganda were all very easy for us to get our hands on. Another song by Skrewdriver, from "Before the Night Falls" in *Hail the New Dawn* album, shows the mentality of the philosophies we began to imbed in our minds and in our hearts:

Our forefathers fought in two world wars, they thought to keep us free
But I'm not sure that in those wars, who was our enemy
The Zionists own the media, and they're known for telling lies
And I could see, that it could be, we fought on the wrong side

While this was obviously a European white power song, we aligned with beliefs and a sense of brotherhood with them. The music and words were powerful—over and over, the lyrics entered our thoughts and our philosophies. Because we were looking for it, we began to see injustice all over the place in America—in government, in business, on the streets, in the jails and court systems. We began to see high-power Jews owning many thriving businesses. We began to see major problems with immigration laws and illegal aliens (easy to do anyway in Southern California, but we twisted everything we saw). We began to imagine that the world was conspiring against us, and that we were soldiers for a bigger cause. What pissed us off was that the rest of the white people around us didn't see what we were doing to clean up America! In fact, they were imprisoning patriots. Here we were, standing against gangs; we were anti-stealing, anti-dopers, and people and the cops were treating us like scumbags, making *us* out to be the bad guys. *We weren't pushing dope on the kids.* We felt like we were the only ones doing anything about people dealing dope in the neighborhoods, black or white or Hispanic. And although the vast majority of people were against these gangbangers and dopers, they were throwing our members in jail. They should be happy we were cleaning up the neighborhood for them. We began to feel aligned with others who were enemies of the state—the KKK, Aryan Resistance, and more.

While becoming openly white power was very dangerous in and of itself (considering the number of powerful ethnic gangs in California), it was the fighting between the factions of Skinheads that were the most deadly. My close friends and I, including Vince, Scott, Derek, Dopey (he had big ears just like the cartoon character), Paul, Danny, and Dave, formed the BBB, or Boot Boy Brotherhood. Our territory controlled everything around the high school and downtown by the mall in Southern Redlands. We did everything we did before joining a gang, but we focused on adding violence to our repertoire of drinking and partying.

The BBB hung out every day, seven days a week, for at least six to eight hours a day. We shifted from rubbing shoulders with punks and multi-ethnic kids at school to Skins and white girls only, and the more racist they were, the better. Even Vince and Dave quit dating their half-Hispanic girlfriends and started dating just Skinhead girls after a while. Some of the BBB were working and some were going to school, but whenever we were not at one of those places we were with each other. It literally was a brotherhood. We were family to each other.

By the time my parents found out about my school situation (or lack thereof), my academics were irretrievable. I'd hardly attended high school at all. My father wouldn't support my lifestyle as generously as he had before I quit school, so I started working at the docks. Of course I got a job that supported my lifestyle. I went to work at three o'clock in the morning, and got off around eleven, in time to pick up my friends that were still in school.

One of BBB's major hangouts was a fast food area at the corner of Redlands Boulevard and Citrus. Everything ebbed and flowed there in this area of town, so it was easy for us to monitor what was happening in our area. It was two blocks from the high school, close to the mall, and a short jaunt down to Main Street. After we had established ourselves, blacks and Hispanics didn't go there except sometimes much older folks or really young, naive individuals, ignorant of the area. As long as they were not gang affiliated, we had no problems. Gangbangers who pushed the limits got the crap beat out of them.

We started getting hard in our beliefs about life, loyalty, and trust. As the stakes became higher and higher in the games we were playing—even to death—we had to rely on each other and know we could trust each other. If anyone broke that trust, they were pretty well black-balled for life. Dopey was a good example of this.

One night Dopey, myself, and a visiting Skin and his girlfriend were hanging out near the entrance to the Redlands mall when a few college boys started making fun of Dopey's ears. To make a long and pitiful story short, Dopey ran away and left us to fight the guys while he "ran to get a security guard." It's interesting to note that while Dopey never once showed cowardice again, we never fully trusted him and never forgave him. Eventually he was ousted from gang life with us altogether. He was a lucky one, because we were new, and we were softies. Most gangs just kill the cowards now.

AMERICAN FIRM: A NEW DAY

During my time with the BBB, so much was happening on the Skinhead scene in California. Smaller Skinhead groups were solidifying with larger groups, which afforded them more protection. The BBB only lasted about a year because American Firm—a better, more organized group—had been formed in Southern California in 1982 and was the premiere group for us to join. Butch, whom we called Ace, was the leader and responsible for putting the gang together. Most of us decided to join him.

While today's young Skins have to commit a horribly violent crime to be let in to the group, when the initiations first began, it was different. The *prospect* was the one who was beaten up, by his brothers in the gang he wanted into. That's what happened to me in 1984.

On a balmy summer night, members of the American Firm and I stopped at a park in La Puente. I knew what was about to happen, because I was a prospect and there was no other reason to stop. I started shaking with anticipation. Adrenaline rushed through me like it never had before.

"Are you ready?" Ace asked me. I swallowed, and nodded. Three guys encircled me. I grabbed one in a big bear hug so he couldn't punch too hard, and I was punching back.

"You have to let go," Ace said. "Your time doesn't start until you *stop* fighting."

I had to take everything they dished out—that was the rule. For two full minutes my buddies proceeded to knock the shit out of me. (That doesn't sound very long until it's happening to you.) It actually wasn't as hard for me as it was for some guys. I was so used to mosh pits. Just like when I was in the middle of one, I was so pumped full of adrenaline that I honestly didn't feel much at all. I was psyched to be a real American Firm member. Vince was jumped in that night, right after me.

Another night a few weeks later, we did a jump-in about two AM. We'd been driving around looking for a park and couldn't find one. Finally we stopped at a grassy area on an elementary school playground. It was time for our new prospects, Chuck and Pete, to be jumped in. Chuck was first. Ace went to shake his hand, grabbed it instead, and with his other fist punched him, hard. Then everyone else jumped in, and we went at it for the conventional couple of minutes. Chuck got up—barely—and it was Pete's turn. We had only been going at Pete for about a minute when we heard this old lady on her telephone, calling the police from her window.

"They're beating another kid!" she yelled shrilly. "They're going to kill him!" Ace punched Pete really hard and the rest of us had one more go and then said, "You're done. Let's get out of here!" We sped away as we heard sirens in the distance, coming fast. We all laughed so hard, and I knew I would never forget that old woman's voice.

Our area was under the leadership of a guy we called Upland Dave (since we knew so many Daves). I was the first BBB member to get jumped in. Since Vince was jumped in on the same night, that made us equals. Anyone we brought in would be under our leadership and direction.

Others from BBB followed as long as they were found worthy. Danny (Eight-Ball), Dave (our other Dave), and Paul joined me. There was a rift between me and Scott, and so he was never allowed to join. Since Dopey had played the coward that night near the mall, he was never allowed in. Under my orders, Derek was jumped in on probation and eventually allowed to be a full member.

I was so pumped about American Firm that I was talking to everybody about it. I got nine guys from RedBoot, four Purdue Skins, and six or seven others who were not affiliated with any Skins group to come into AF right away. In a short time, Vince and I went from being lower members on the totem pole to leadership positions, since the guys I brought in had to answer to me. Vince brought in Derek and another kid, the Clown. In a way, Vince was really under me, because I had brought in twenty guys while he brought in two. With me doing all this recruiting, it pushed Upland Dave into second in charge. Within about six months I went from being a member of BBB to being third in charge of the American Firm in Southern California. I only had to answer to Upland Dave and to Ace.

As part of the American Firm, my buddies and I continued to take on more beliefs similar to the original Nazis of World War II. We literally began to believe in and support the world expansion and domination of the white race. Our main goal became elimination of the Jew from the world. Of course we included a few other enemies in there as well, like blacks, homosexuals, physically challenged people, and so forth. We also began to hate white people who were *not* racist because they were all traitors. We hated everybody who was mentally or physically disabled. Essentially, anybody who was not white power became our enemy.

Strangely enough, however, our biggest enemy for several years turned out to be other Skinheads. California had become interlaced with some of the most dangerous gangs known in its history. Despite looking for opportunities to commit hate crimes, most of our aggression was carried out against other Skinheads. While hate and violence *were* rampant among racial groups, it was nothing compared to what we did to each other during the Skinhead Wars. In fact, during my entire career as a Skinhead, 90 percent of my victims were *white*.

The Skinhead Wars had begun.

5

SUDDEN ENEMY

AS SOON AS I was jumped into the American Firm in the summer of 1984, I became the sudden and sworn enemy to all the rest of the Skinheads—even those I had been great buddies with for the last eighteen months.

Our main enemy was American Front, Skinheads whose territories overlapped with ours. It was sometimes confusing, with names so closely aligned (and the same acronym: AF), with members often living in the same town, both claiming the territories as their own.

In addition, wherever Skins had a girlfriend, that territory automatically became their area. Since Skinhead relationships were often volatile, the next week a girl might begin dating someone from the other group, and territorial claims could get crazy. For example, one week we would claim San Gabriel Valley and the next week American Front would.

One of the main problems I encountered was in attending concerts or hanging out with friends in new areas. When we spotted a group of Skinheads dressed exactly like us, we'd have no more than ten seconds to determine if they were American Front or American Firm. If there were only a couple of us and a bunch of them and we caught a glimpse of an American Front patch, we'd spew cusswords at them and run like hell in the opposite direction. If there were more of us and only a few of them, odds were in the favor of them receiving a good beating.

As with any group that grows rapidly in such a short period of time, there were bugs to be worked out within the Skinhead ranks, even as we struggled to remain tight against our enemies. One night I found out that

Danny's brother Paul, the Clown, and Ronnie had all been jumped into AF without my knowledge by other members of the Firm. I knew these guys personally, and they were living in my area. I was furious. There were reasons I hadn't yet jumped them in. I felt like I should have known about it—actually been informed about it *before* it happened. When Upland Dave found out, he became almost as furious as me. There were issues of trust going on here, as well as politics and power.

"You *must* check with us before jumping anyone in our territory," Upland Dave ordered Ace. "Those who hadn't been jumped in yet were still prospects because they were not worthy." What Dave didn't add was if someone was worthy, we damn well wanted them jumped in *under* us to become part of *our* power and ranks.

"*I* run this area—" Ace began.

"Yeah, but you don't know these guys. I'm telling you, they don't deserve membership." A big silence greeted Upland Dave, and then a sigh sounded from the other end of the phone.

"What do you want to do?" Ace asked, resignedly.

"Put them on probation," I said, "until we know they've earned it."

Ace reluctantly agreed.

That weekend, we went to another party at Regina's house. Regina had dated some Skinhead guys from time to time. She often had parties at her house, and it was a fun place to hang out. She was super cool, super cute, and we all had crushes on her at one time or another. While she was not associated with the Movement, she had been friends with most of us for a long, long time. Paul, the Clown, and Ronnie were hanging out.

"Heads up, guys," I said. "This is my territory. Therefore, the decisions I make affect you. We talked to Ace and told him we're putting you guys on probation. You're not full-fledged members until I say you are."

"Hey, that's not fair!" they all protested.

"Give me your freakin' sweatshirts, or go along with it!" I looked at each guy in the eye until he looked away. "Anyone have a problem with that?" They all said no, because no one really wanted to mess with me.

Paul and the Clown became full-fledged members, but not Ronnie. I caught Ronnie smoking pot one night, and he had no choice but to admit it.

"I want your sweatshirt NOW!" I snarled. "Don't come around here again, don't claim affiliation with any Skins, and you're not to have anything to do with any of us!"

Once banned, detested, and excluded, the drug scene had infiltrated Skinheads and this type of altercation started happening all the time. It made me physically ill. This wasn't what being a Skinhead stood for. I felt like we should beat up drug pushers and put them behind bars or in the ground, not become them.

In order to continue the fast-paced, violent lifestyle I had become accustomed to, I found I needed a lot more money. Dad gave me money— he gave me *a lot* of money, actually—but I needed more for all the gas, weapons, alcohol, concerts, and girlfriends. In addition, I was bringing in all kinds of kids to join under us in the American Firm. Some were rich kids and some were poor kids. Vince and I would pull some cash together and go over to a shop at the Redlands Mall where we always had our sweatshirts made. In old English letters, "American Firm Skinheads" was emblazoned across the back. The shoulder said, "U.S. Skin." Once a kid was jumped in, we would give him a sweatshirt during a special ceremony. Between that and giving away boots and other clothing items, I racked up even more expenses.

We were always looking for ways to get cash. Since the majority of us original Skins had quit doing drugs when we joined the Skinheads, we believed that drug dealers were the scum of the earth. Therefore, it was easy to justify getting drunk and beating up drug dealers to take their money. Unfortunately, it was a dangerous game and didn't always create enough cash.

I got a new job at a fast food restaurant in Redlands. Just like at home, by day I made myself out to be a conservative middle-class kid, and I worked a good forty hours every week. Like my parents, my bosses had no idea what kind of lifestyle I led at night. I kept my gang tattoos hidden and my views to myself, and no one bothered me about it. While my job helped with cash flow, it didn't fully satisfy my need for more money.

We were all in a similar situation, so American Firm developed a plan that went right with our philosophy and our hungry wallets. One night we went into West Hollywood to a place that we knew was solicited primarily by gay men. We had Little Davy stand outside the bar. He simply kicked back out front until a guy walked up and started talking to him. Then the man began hitting on him. Two of us were positioned across the street in the shadows, watching their every move.

"I've never done this before," Little Davy said shyly. "Can we go somewhere private?"

The man motioned down and around the corner to where his car was parked. My buddy and I took off, running down the street, around the corner, and through the alleyway where they would be headed momentarily. A couple of our other associates were already there.

"Little Davy is on his way," we said, warning them. My adrenaline had shifted into high gear.

When the two of them came around and into the parking lot, the gay guy motioned toward a car. When they were a full fifteen to twenty feet off the main road and out of sight of most passersby, we bum-rushed the gay man and beat the crap out of him, speaking as unkindly as possible while trying not to draw any attention to ourselves.

"We know who you are, you fag!" we said, terrorizing him. We took his wallet, kicked him a few additional times, and took off long before anybody noticed us. All of this happened just three blocks from the West Hollywood Police Department. We knew he would never tell the authorities. There was never a lot of sympathy from cops about that sort of thing. This victim never told a soul, and we got away, free to do it again to someone else. We took fagbashing to an entirely new level.

Our simple plan worked every time. We would send one of our young, attractive boys outside of a bar in West Hollywood, San Bernardino, Riverside, or another area we knew they were likely to get picked up. Some of our gutsier boys would go in and get a drink until someone hit on him. Either way, it didn't matter. Older gay men always seemed to carry a lot of cash, and the whole thing worked because to our knowledge, none of them ever called the police or told anyone in authority what had happened.

WHICH WHITE MAKES RIGHT?

One night, our brother Danny was shot in the San Gabriel Valley by members of American Front. I have rarely been as angry as I was that night, and my buddies were all in the same spirit of assassination. Upland Dave, Bullet, a couple other Firm guys, and I went driving around West Covina looking for Front members. We found two unfortunate members by themselves. Catching them by complete surprise, we ganged up on them using a bully bat, a golf club, our boots, and whatever else was at our disposal. Even when they were down and unconscious, we beat them and kicked them several more times before we took off.

Not surprisingly, a few nights later when Bullet was sitting on a bench waiting for a bus in La Puente, some Front members ran up on him and stabbed him in the upper torso, trying to kill him. From that point on, I always had a weapon with me. I didn't go anywhere without my knife, bully bat, chains, and brass knuckles. Shortly thereafter, I purchased my first firearm.

The fighting between American Firm and American Front actually caused a power struggle within our tightly knit Skins. After Bullet got stabbed, Upland Dave and I figured the only way to pay back American Front was to kill one of them. We brought it up to Ace.

"No," disagreed Ace. He was adamant. "You can't do it. I won't allow it."

"I don't think Ace is up to the challenge of leadership," Upland Dave said. "Our chapter and our affiliates are growing stronger, and we've taken control of the Inland Empire, all because we are NOT afraid." Dave started to push Ace out of leadership. Bit by bit, the rift grew larger and larger. Then one night at a party, Upland Dave called Ace out.

"I'm no longer following you," Dave said, his face grim. "You're out of the gang. You're through!" Ace stared at him with a cold, ugly glare that would make most people's blood run cold.

"I'm not going," Ace said. Dave realized at that moment he would have to kill him to get him out of leadership. Ace had started American Firm and had been in for a long time. He also had some pretty loyal associates. Little Davy, Bullet, and some others stuck by Ace, and American Firm split up into two groups.

For the next few years, Californians were the victim of the onslaught of a huge rise in gang offenses and hate crimes. There were sharp increases in muggings, drive-by shootings, and slashings. All manner of hate crimes were published in the papers during this time. California did not have a hate crime law yet, or even a bill in the House. The Skinhead Wars and their vicious fallout caused legislation to be drafted and enacted very quickly.

THE BOY WHO CRIED BB GUN

While the biggest challenges with other gangs remained American Front and other Skins, we had occasional skirmishes with ethnic gangs. Our biggest nemesis in that category was a group called MMM, the Mighty Mod Mafia, or Mods, as we called them. They dressed like the sixties, rode scooters, jammed to reggae, and had their own style of clothing. One group of multi-ethnic Mods called themselves the Rude Boys. These Mods dressed more like Skinheads, but of course were often black or multi-ethnic. We got to know Roger, a black guy, and Danny Boy, a white boy who was with them. They started hanging around our territory, causing trouble, and they were flashing their colors. They let everyone know they were anti-racist and tagged MMM all over.

A girl I had dated for quite a while hooked up with Danny Boy. My buddies and I called her several unsavory names that jealous boys often said about girls. Danny Boy felt like he had to stand up for her. He let me know he wanted to talk to me. I invited him over to my mom's house. Vince, Eight-Ball, and I then hung out at my mom's house while she was at work. Roger and Danny Boy knocked on the door. Eight-Ball answered.

"I want to talk to TJ," Danny Boy said, a little nervous.

"You can come in," said Eight-Ball, "but your pet has to stay outside." He was referring to Roger. My boys and I all started laughing. Danny Boy came over to the table, where Vince and I were sitting.

"I heard you been saying stuff about my girl," he said gruffly.

"Yeah," I said, "so what? If truth hurts, truth hurts."

"You get to stop talking trash, because if you don't, I have to defend her, and that's going to cause problems."

"I don't care," I said. "If that's what it's going to be, it's going to be."

Danny and I both felt the tension in the room grow bigger and bigger.

"You're safe," I said. "I invited you over."

Danny backed up to the door, watching us carefully.

"I guess we're going to have to go to war," he said as he and Roger left.

Later on that night, we heard that those two were driving around in a Volkswagen bus. They drove up on Dopey and Derek who were walking down the street. One of them flashed a gun from the bus and aimed at them. There were no shots fired, but Dopey and Derek hit the ground and the guys drove away. As soon as we got the whole story, Scott suddenly called us, saying that they had done the same thing to him in his front yard. They didn't know who they were messing with. We started to load up our gear.

While we were getting ready to go out looking for these guys, a girl we knew who worked at Jack in the Box called to inform us that they were parked in the restaurant parking lot. Danny went to his brother's house while Derek and Dopey took Vince to his house to get weapons. In the meantime, I walked downtown a block and half. I didn't want to be in my car because I was packing. I had my new 9mm cocked and ready to go. I secretly hoped they would pull what they had done to the others on me and I could just light up their bus. I was out for real vengeance.

Becoming more wary as I got nearer, I positioned myself at an angle where I could see the Jack-in-the-Box and the bus, still parked there. I started walking very quickly, in order to rush across the street and get in better position before I made my presence known.

Just then, the entire Redlands Police Department screamed around every corner and surrounded the VW bus. They pulled Danny Boy, Roger, and another kid out and started searching the vehicle. I was watching in fascination when Danny pulled up. I covertly handed him my gun.

"Go up to Regina's house and hole up there till I get there," I ordered, then I shuffled across the street.

I stood by the growing crowd and watched everything. The officers pulled the gun out, and I couldn't believe it. These Rude Boys had a BB gun of all things! One of the guys had taken the barrel off the gun to make it look more real and menacing. All I can say is they were lucky the police came when they did. If not, there would have been three dead people in that bus.

They were arrested and booked on charges. I went up to Regina's house where everyone was hanging out. The boys died laughing when they heard the MMM members were caught with a BB gun. Serious word got out to Danny Boy, Roger, and the Rude Boys that they had been within ten minutes of losing their lives. They never came back to town. They vanished, like magic. That's when we started going to MMM parties in San Bernardino and tearing it up.

One night soon after the Mods' arrest, we drove to a party where we knew some really cute girls and MMM members were hanging out. The place was filled with mostly younger kids. We drove over, and we must've looked really sinister just by walking in the door. One of the MMM leaders spoke up quickly.

"Look, guys, we don't want no trouble. No trouble."

"Fine," we said, grabbing cups and drinking out of their keg.

Within just a couple of minutes of our arrival, the police showed up to break up the party. We smiled at the police in our friendly, good citizens' performance, picked up the keg, and strode off with it. Not one MMM member said a thing; they just watched us carry it out the door.

SUCKERS FOR CONSPIRACY

One of the major reasons hate crimes steadily increased in California was because Skins and other racist gangs became more indoctrinated in separatist principles and propaganda. We sent away for materials and received an overwhelming response. Hate pamphlets and white power music were cheap. We wrote and spoke on the phone with powerful white separatists like Dr. William Pierce, who wrote the *Turner Diaries* under the pseudonym Andrew McDonald; Michael Hoffman, who wrote *Candidate for the Order* and other separatist, racist materials; and Tom Metzger, editor and publisher of *WAR* (White Aryan Resistance) newspaper. They told us all about organized rallies and summer camps we could go to, to learn more about hatred, violence, and how to destroy America.

From the propaganda we received, we "learned" that the conspirator dogs (Jews) had taken over, that our government was secretly aligned with Israel, that the United Nations was part of the conspiracy, and that the World Bank (owned by Jews, of course) would soon rule the world. We became angrier at the injustice that was happening in the world. We wanted to annihilate anyone who stood in the way of a truly free America: all Jews, Hispanics, blacks, mixed-race mongrels, and homosexuals were our targeted victims. Dr. William Pierce's quote, "Euthanized or sterilized," was our idea of a great time on any given night of the week. We ate up the propaganda like it was candy—the sweet and sour kind.

One day in the early hours of a morning, I was finishing up some rigorous tasks at my job at the fast food restaurant in Redlands. I had worked all night because we had a big inspection the next day. I had been sharing some Bacardi with two friends and took the rest of the bottle with me as I went out to my car. I was alone in the parking lot when another vehicle drove up with a bunch of Hispanic guys, a couple of which I knew from RLS, or South Side Redlands. Our two gangs had tolerated each other fairly well up until that point. These guys were all friendly and asked me to come and see something.

As I approached the car, I had no clue that earlier that night, my buddies had jumped one of their friends and beat him brutally. Cell phones were not as available as they are today, or I would have been warned. As it was, I just leaned into the car when suddenly a knife flashed toward my face. I put my hands up to protect myself, and the guy sliced the palm of my left hand before I could back away. I felt like I had put my hand on a hot grill. Then it instantly turned cold. I turned my hand over in shock to see a huge gash, and my cupped fingers quickly filled with blood. The RLS members sped away, leaving me with my dripping wound.

The knife had completely cut a nerve and sliced the tendon in half, but I would live. I staggered inside to my bosses, already making up a good excuse. I told them I had picked up a Bacardi bottle in the parking lot, and on my way to throw it out I had tripped and fallen on the bottle. They freaked out and were ready to call an ambulance. I told them to call my dad instead—he'd get there quicker because we lived only two blocks away. I also knew better than to mess with a 911 call. There would be too many questions asked. I watched nervously as they bandaged my hand in a white towel. Within seconds the towel was soaked and dripping with blood. I went outside to wait for Dad—and to avoid any more questions. When my dad pulled up, he raced me to the hospital, probing me with questions that made me uncomfortable the whole way. Still, once we got there, he seemed to believe my story.

Fortunately for me, they called in a terrific hand surgeon to take care of me. I think they were motivated because even after the staff washed the cut out and put pressure on it, it continued to bleed profusely. The bad news was this doc was a little too smart. He asked me how I had cut my hand so badly, and I told him the story about the Bacardi bottle. He looked at me strangely and said, "Glass doesn't cut like this." My dad got mad and demanded the truth. I knew the cops would be there the minute I spoke the truth of what really happened. Instead, I stuck by my earlier story. The surgeon shook his head and said it was the cleanest bottle cut he'd ever seen in his life. He completed the hand surgery, and I walked out with eighteen stitches. My work paid for my medical bills. I was only eighteen years old, no longer a fresh-cut boot or green Skinhead. I'd been through a lot, and I knew all the rules, including "no snitching." You take care of your problems yourself.

I never went back to work at the restaurant. I didn't feel it was safe there anymore. That situation and the growing tension between Skins and ethnic gangs further entrenched me into my racist beliefs. It also made me paranoid. I realized that I didn't want my little brothers, Mat and Phil, to get involved in American Firm—or any other gang, for that matter. If people didn't like you, they could easily kill you. I began to worry more and more about my little brothers. They liked hanging out with me sometimes, and my lifestyle probably seemed a little glamorous to them. Phil, luckily, had only shown up at a few parties (but never solid Skinhead shows). Mat was another story.

One night a few months after my stabbing, Mat showed up at a straight Skinhead party in Redlands all dressed in black. Black is a prospect color, the flashing of a wannabe.

"You've got to leave now," I said. I steered him toward the door.

"What is your problem?" he asked, confused. "I have every right to be here. You do this. You're into it. Why can't I?"

"You don't know what this all involves," I said. It was true. He had no idea! He saw the parties, the drinking, the girls, but he didn't know. *None of my family really knew.* I was determined that I wouldn't lose my little brother to gang violence.

"Get out of here, NOW," I said menacingly. "And don't you ever come back. I will kick the crap out of you at every party you show up to."

Enraged, Mat left. I didn't give him a choice. He knew I *would* knock him out cold until he got the idea.

It was 1985—a very volatile year. We had knives and guns everywhere we went—in our cars, on our bodies, at our parties, even in our own homes. I had been with people in drive-by beatings before and even in drive-by shootings, but I participated in my first drive-by shooting that year, hitting a target with my own gun. I will never forget that night.

The event went by in a blur, and while some details I can't recall so clearly, others are firmly etched in my mind, and the consequences of the bullets flashing out of my gun—did I actually hit the kid or not? As we drove home I was shaking and had to hold my stomach in check around the guys so they wouldn't know I was about to vomit at any moment. I couldn't sleep that night, or the night after, or even the night after. Instead, I was a nervous wreck, checking the news and the obituaries every day for several days afterward to see if he had died. I never discovered the answer—the consequences of the bullets that came from my own gun.

After that, a stone cold began to fill me. I became less and less afraid because I simply began not feeling at all. The more violent we became, the more shootings and stabbings that we participated in, the more I became cold and numb to fear, and especially to other people's feelings. Once I stabbed the next kid, I didn't care. By the second or third drive-by shooting, it was no longer any big deal. My whole train of thought totally changed. I was past the point of feeling anything—anything—even when guys were much larger than me and it seemed my chances were slim.

I ran my own gang unit of American Firm in Redlands, and as a leader, my responsibility was to be the example, to show the way. I knifed two kids that year, and I can't count the number of drive-bys I led against other Skins. We were on our guard at all times, in every situation. The lessons I had learned at my cousin Bobbie's house served me well. *You are never safe. There is nowhere to run, nowhere to hide. Be on guard at every minute, for danger is always just around the corner or perhaps right behind you. When fighting erupts, dig in fast and do as much damage as quickly as possible. Leave chaos in your wake to establish a reputation bigger than you, for that alone just might save your life.*

The coldness that filled me pushed away any compassion that I once may have had. I began to say and do things that would have been impossible only a year or two before, when I had feelings. At a party one evening, a Berdo Skin (from San Bernardino) threatened to commit a drive-by shooting at my house. I looked him right in the eye and said, "You will regret that for the rest of your life, because I will butcher your mom and your brother and everyone right in front of you." My energy told him everything he needed to know, and he backed off. The frightening thing is that I really would have.

Another night at a party, I told an opponent that I had never lost a gang fight, and that I never would.

"You might beat me," I said, "but I'll come back and blow your knees off." He stared at me.

"That's not cool," he said, melodramatically. "That's not even slightly fair."

"I could care less," I said, quite serious. "Just know that I will do whatever it takes to win. I will take every necessary step to bring you down."

In my mind, every battle was war, and the winners were those willing to do whatever it took, not only to survive but to come out on top. Straight out of the history books, it was a Machiavellian attitude: The end justifies the means. Taking a page out of alternate history books and white power fiction like *The Turner Diaries, Candidate for the Order*, and *Hear the Cradle Song*, I felt justified in whatever actions gave me exactly what I desired in order to follow the Movement. The only feelings I held were the feelings of being unstoppable.

Within a year, the Skins in Redlands, Highlands, and Yucaipa were all under my jurisdiction, even as we ventured out further into San Bernardino. Our Firm groups were becoming larger and stronger, making it possible to progress further and further out. As Upland Dave's sergeant, I was recruiting all kinds of kids into American Firm. They answered to me, and I eventually took over three other cities: Colton, Rialto, and Fontana, my home town.

Look at me now, I thought.

6

RISING FORCE

BY 1987, I started heavily inking my body with Skinhead emblems. I started with a small, sinister-looking swastika and a set of lightning bolts. This was just the beginning of the Aryan, white power, and racist symbols I would use to decorate my body. Next I had "Skins Rip" (meaning Skins are number one) and DCHC (Deadlands County Hard-core) tattooed on my arms and back, along with three skulls, just for effect. My favorite skull had a confederate bandana on it. Finally, on my lower calve I tattooed a black swastika. Most of my tattoos were given by friends or created in tattoo shops after hours. I only paid for the first one or two tattoos during my entire Skinhead career.

Every tatt stood for something, and several had been earned through violent behavior against others. They were a confirmation of my reputation and my willingness to cross all lines of authority. Like my fellow Skins, I attacked anyone who I perceived as different. My race became my religion.

Every night, everywhere we went, my gang and I were packing guns, knives, and enough ammo to take down the Alamo. I always had my 9mm pistols with me. At times, I got a weird feeling—fast, strong, and shocking. The tension had become almost palpable every night we went out, and we were out every night. Something inside me inherently knew what we were doing was wrong, but eventually I came to believe so heavily in the cause that it didn't matter. I was a soldier for the Movement, and I was committed to my very core.

By this point, everything I did contributed to a deeper cycle of indoctrination into racism. The more I tattooed myself with racist images, the more I showed them off to my friends and associates. The more I read the white power propaganda, the more I bought into the messages I read. Every night as I partied to hate-filled, white power music, the more solidly I identified with the messages that I was hearing, creating, and experiencing. I was the angry white man with the semi-automatic, ready to blow off the head of any Jew, black, or race traitor that stepped into my path. In fact, I was always loaded and ready for action for the race war I believed was coming.

I had come to believe that Jews really were the spawn of Satan and that they had developed a worldwide conspiracy. While there was too much evidence to the contrary, I wanted to believe the revisionists who said the Holocaust was a bold-faced lie. I utilized and twisted that information to my benefit. I told my soldiers that more than six million Jews had not honestly been killed—their deaths and those of millions of others were a disgraceful sham that forced a compassionate United States to give Israel millions and millions of dollars every year. I fully embraced the belief that the world's capital would become established in Tel Aviv, and Jews would control the earth unless we did something to stop them.

What fascinated me about separatist and racist propaganda is the fact that both white and black separatists use a lot of the *same* material. In fact, when separatism became really big among black nationalists, white and black separatists held meetings *together* to discuss their literature and come to an agreement on the most powerful language. If you take out the word *white* and replace it with *black*, you have literally the same separatist, racist language that works for both groups. The same works for Hispanic and Latino separatists. No matter their own skin color, separatists believe in building power through separation until enough power is accumulated for total annihilation of everyone else. They're preaching the same message, just to a different color audience.

Another interesting and compelling fact to me was that white power wasn't backed by a bunch of rednecks in the woods. There were doctors, lawyers, ministers, and even software moguls behind the cause! I remember reading the words of William Pierce, who had a doctorate in physics: "Today it finally began! After all these years of talking—and nothing but talking—we have finally taken our first action. We are at war with the system, and it is no longer a war of words."

This stuck with me. It was very powerful. Dr. Pierce was the leader of the National Alliance, one of the largest neo-Nazi organizations in the world. He was also the one who wrote *The Turner Diaries* under a pen name. This is the book that inspired Tim McVeigh to bomb the federal building in Oklahoma City. McVeigh also believed Pierce's rhetoric that Jews and race traitors should be "euthanized or sterilized."

I was so excited about the Movement; I was constantly recruiting more and more kids to join. For whatever reason, many people listened to me. Of course, not all of them believed what I had to teach, and so I read as many recruiting techniques as I could find in the white power literature. I dropped anything that wasn't effective, and I quickly adopted anything that worked.

Once I recruited a kid, it didn't matter if he was a loner or popular among his peers—I had uses for every kid. Loners were easy to pull in because they usually had a chip on their shoulder that no one else had helped them in overcoming. We were there for them. We were family. In turn, they became loyal beyond belief, especially because they literally had nowhere else to go. A popular kid, on the other hand, was an added bonus, because I could suck in his friends almost effortlessly.

One of my favorite techniques was to make copies of a Screwdriver album like *Blood & Honour,* or *Boots & Braces* to share with anyone who would listen. I knew that no matter how cool a flyer was that we developed with racist information, I would be lucky if a kid hung onto it for more than a day. However, if I gave a kid a tape of music and he dug the sound, he would listen to it a hundred times over. Often even more. I also knew the lyrics would roll unconsciously around and around in his mind for hours after the music was shut off. It would begin to weedle its way into the brain and become ingrained either subtly or boldly as new beliefs. Some of the songs I would give them had lyrics like these, found on an album entitled *White Power*:

> *I stand, watch my country, going down the drain*
> *We are all at fault, we are all to blame*
> *We're letting them take over, we just let 'em come*
> *Once we had an Empire, and now we've got a slum*
>
> *Well we've seen a lot of riots, we just sit and scoff*
> *We've seen a lot of muggings, and the judges let 'em off*
> *Well we've gotta do something, to try and stop the rot*
> *And the traitors that have used us, they should all be shot*

From the album *Get on the Boat*:

Nigger, nigger, get on that boat, Nigger, nigger, row
Nigger, nigger, get out of here, Nigger, nigger, go, go, go . . .

We've got to love this land of ours, and fight to keep it white
Never going to give it up, 'cause we know we're in the right
And if they try to take it, we will fight them to the death
And in the end, the white man wins, 'cause there won't be no rest

Ian Stewart (Donaldson), lead singer of Skrewdriver—and once the singer in a warm-up band that toured with the Rolling Stones—was instrumental in getting the Skinhead Movement going in Europe and bringing it to the United States. Skrewdriver's hits were popular with all the U.S. Skins (except SHARPs, of course) and spread heavily throughout California, as well as wherever the Movement was growing throughout the United States. It had a hard-hitting, addictive beat. Usually once I gave some kids this free music, they wanted more.

"Hey, you got some more of that music, man?" they would say, smirking a bit. Lots of times they thought they were pulling wool over my eyes. I'd just smile widely.

"Sure!" I'd say, and hand out more. We loved giving them *Boots & Braces*. Pretty soon, several of them would be shaving their heads, pulling on Doc Martens, and showing up at parties, dressed in black.

Boots and braces, shaven-headed hoards
Boots and braces, fighting 'cause you're bored
Boots and braces, you'll always get the blame
Boots and braces, we'll come in just the same
Wearing your Ben Sherman in the sun
Trying to figure out just who to run
Levi jeans, Doc Marten boots, and just hear the Skinhead roar—Skinhead!
No one stands against us, 'cause we've beat 'em all before

Black Flag, an American band from Los Angeles, seemed to carry on the same racist energy in their song "White Minority." Some music historians claim that the song is actually an attack on white supremacy, a mockery of racism. (Chavo Pederast, lead singer, was part-Hispanic, another player was a big BB King fan, and another was Colombian born. In addition, the band's producer was black.) However, the song was passed around like it was racist, used like it was racist, and got kids fired up like any Skrewdriver song. We used any tool we could get our hands on, and it didn't matter the source.

Gonna be a white minority
There's gonna be large casualty
Within my new territory
You're all gonna die

I found that hatred was an easy thing to sell to confused teenage kids. Like me, so many of them were filled with anger and hatred already. Recruiting them to become thugs was a breeze. A lot of kids off the street just wanted protection. A growing number of them were being pushed around by the rising Hispanic and black gangs, especially in certain areas of the state. Eventually, they'd shave their heads and hang out with us. It's interesting to note that none of these kids started out as hard-core. It would only take us about a year, and hard-core is exactly what they would be.

Drunk with power, I loved turning certain kids against each other in power plays to make them loyal very quickly. I loved the power, control, and influence I exerted over so many. I could get them to do whatever I wanted them to do for me—even kill for me.

For example, one night I made a remark in an offhand manner. I never gave an order, I never even looked at anyone in the face, much less winked or raised a brow. (In other words, no evidence could be construed against me.)

"That house needs a freakin' lesson," I said flippantly. The next thing I knew, the guy's house had been lit up like a Christmas tree, bullets raining everywhere. I wasn't anywhere around. I didn't have to be. Yet I was the man with the power.

A couple of months later, the Skins were having a huge party for the Inland Empire to clear up some of the hard feelings that had developed between the two factions within American Firm. Ace had been pushed out of the number one spot, though he was still a leader in his own right. Upland Dave and I, along with Ace, Big Davy, and Gabriel, created a council. If anything happened, it had to go before the Council. We agreed there would be three votes on the Council: Ace, Gabriel, and Upland Dave. The balance of power had shifted, but there were no more hard feelings. We were free to progress again, and more important, all members of

American Firm could rely on each other again. Instead of worrying about being stabbed in the back (literally), we were watching each other's backs once more. It also gave Upland Dave and I incredible, undisputed power over our own ranks.

One day I arrived at my mom's pumped full of adrenaline. I had recruited two new Skins, our territorial disputes were being settled, and we were having a landmark year. Filled with happiness, I started spouting some of my growing white power beliefs to my brothers. They blew me off, saying what an idiot I was. I really didn't care. They were safe, and I still was who I was. I made the mistake of simply mentioning a bit of racist crap to my mom, and she wouldn't hear another second of it.

"Don't talk to me about that stuff!" she yelled, her hands over her ears, her eyes defiant. "I don't want to hear any more!"

Despite my beliefs that had twisted away so dramatically from my family's, my brothers and my mother always invited me over for family get-togethers and activities. They continued to embrace me, just not my philosophies. I think they all thought it was a phase I would simply get over soon.

CAUGHT AND CORNERED

We three boys ended up living at my mother's small two-bedroom apartment in Redlands. She was in one room while Mat, Phil, and I were crammed in the other bedroom. It was often a complete mess. As usual, Mom's room and the rest of the place was meticulously clean and tidy. Phil had stayed with my mom through the entire divorce process and beyond. Though Mat and I had lived off and on with our dad, it always seemed to involve so much drama. In addition to his depressions and suicide attempts, we weren't always welcome. He seemed to want us to live with him when there were child support issues, or to make himself look like the good guy, but unless there was a current issue, it simply wasn't convenient.

In the meantime, I had gone back to working at the docks. I had been loading and unloading diesels with a forklift and by hand, which kept me in really great shape. Working at the docks with me were two other white guys and a Hispanic kid. The rule was that if you were late for work, you had to stop and buy everyone donuts. I was so often late I generally stopped for donuts several times a week, since I usually went straight to work after partying. Eventually I thought I should take up a financial interest in the donut shop.

After a particularly exhausting day at work, I came home in desperate need of a shower. I had always kept my tattoos covered, and my mother had never seen them. My brothers had glimpsed a few of them, but since I had kept them out of the Movement, it wasn't a big deal. They knew of my reputation, but they didn't understand the violent symbolism behind every tattoo. Stripping down in the bathroom, I realized I had forgotten my clean shirt in my room. I quickly ran down the hall in just a towel to grab my shirt and then headed back.

When I heard the gasp of horror, I knew that I'd been caught. For years now, I had been able to hide the depth of my involvement in the racist movement from my mother. Until now, she didn't really have a clue about how far I had become entrenched into the world of hate.

"What are those?" she cried, her voice shrill and tight. She pointed at my body, covered from my neck to the middle of my back in graphic, sinister tattoos. "What do those mean?"

There was no way in hell I was going to tell her what they meant—the hate crimes I had committed, the people I'd hurt, stabbed, and maimed to earn those tattoos. No way would I tell her about all the other kids I'd initiated to follow me and become Skinheads. I pulled my shirt on in defiant silence.

"You tell me," she threatened, "or I'm calling the police!" I shrugged. As if the police could stop me. No one had ever stopped me from doing exactly what I had wanted to do for the last five years—at least not for more than a day or two. She picked up the phone, her eyes locked on mine. I leaned up against the wall while they connected her to the gang unit of the Redlands Police Department. She questioned the officer about what she had seen, and her eyes grew bigger in disbelief as he explained what the tattoos meant—in detail. I could hear enough to know this guy knew some of his stuff, but I showed no emotion, even as he told her that the person she was asking about must be a fully indoctrinated and active Skinhead. Then he asked the inevitable question. Did she know this dangerous person she had seen with the tattoos? Was she in any danger?

"It's my son, TJ Leyden," she admitted, her lips trembling. Hot tears of shame, frustration, and panic were running down her cheeks.

"You're kidding, right?" the officer asked incredulously. "*The* TJ Leyden? Is this a prank?"

"No!" she cried. "It's my son, and I deserve to know exactly what he's involved in."

The officer proceeded to tell her that I belonged to a local gang of Skins called American Firm. Of course, he then proceeded to add that I was an active recruiter, bringing in new people under me all the time—teaching them how to fight, how to hate. He even went so far as to tell her that they had suspicions of my involvement in multiple violent acts and hate crimes, but that they had no direct evidence—yet. He said I was on the top of their list.

"What I'm telling you," he said determinedly, "is that your son TJ is a powerful leader of one of the most dangerous gangs of Skinheads in the nation."

At that point, my mother got off the phone and collapsed against the wall. Before I could react, however, she steeled herself, and without looking at me, marched determinedly past me into my room, looking around carefully. With great deliberation, she grabbed all my paraphernalia—any stuff that looked suspicious to her—and threw it right into the garbage. She didn't say much to me except that my "Nazi friends" were not welcome in her apartment any longer. I don't think she knew what else to say. She seemed as angry at herself as she was at me.

Out of respect for her, I didn't bring any Skin brothers or racist stuff around, except every once in a while when I knew she was going to be gone. Neither she nor I mentioned this incident, my tattoos, or my beliefs again for quite some time. Still, that incident did not keep me from becoming increasingly involved with the Movement.

My mother never knew the signs. While she did get a leg up on the tattoos, she didn't know what it meant when I wore my braces down, or what the color of laces on my Doc Marten boots stood for. She didn't understand the racist lingo and the coded language of the Skins, which had become eerily similar to other white supremacist organizations. There was so much she didn't know . . . and I left her there, in the dark.

7

The Heat Is On

IT HADN'T TAKEN me long to get noticed by the biggest, smartest animals in the business. I was damn good at recruiting into the Movement, as well as finding and disseminating information by other groups. The KKK, Aryan Nation, White Aryan Resistance (WAR), and others began noticing the Skinhead Movement, and they were noticing me, since I was the one always requesting information, and I would utilize whatever they sent. I also was the one who wrote and sent in articles to whatever publications they might have.

Many of the older, more established groups wanted mature Skinheads who had "grown up." They thought perhaps I would be the mouthpiece for them. Leadership in these groups felt there was too much violence and immaturity involved in most Skinhead activities and that it was spoiling the broader message by resolving the minds of communities against white power, instead of for it. They were also uncomfortable with the fact that so many of us were loosely banded. They knew we were loaded guns, ready to go off half-cocked at just about anything, which was very true. Somehow, they wanted us to embrace the Aryan Movement and join together in a worldwide brotherhood of solidarity and power. Tom Metzger was one of the first who saw the potential to use our energy for a bigger cause than single, meaningless hate-crimes. He and the others had a bigger vision.

Despite their desire for us to "grow up," not one of the leaders could overlook the power that Skinheads controlled. Especially when they wanted something to get done (a crime that needed to be committed), they knew we wouldn't flinch. If they had a legitimate target, we were the relatives, the brothers that could assist them in their dirty work. Oftentimes we did, although these ventures we all kept to ourselves, of course. Whenever they could, they published our more public feats in the Aryan magazines, and they gave us a lot more notoriety.

"School Gets Hit with Racist Flyers!" the paper would say. "Racial Tensions on Campus at All-time High" and "Skinheads Attack Local Synagogues."

We would share these stories with local prospects every chance we got.

"Look! We made the *WAR* newspaper!" we'd shout, thinking we had earned bragging rights. We'd show them our pictures and articles and make out how cool we were. Or we'd have them listen to Tom Metzgar's hotline when he had a message about our activities. He would say that to find out more about our activities, we were the ones to contact in our area, and give out our information.

The Skinhead Movement was still in its infancy and spreading through California like wildfire. While it seemed like I was such a big mover and shaker, the reality was that I was weirdly in the right place at the right time for recruiting purposes. I had a lot of time on my hands and would run into other gangs frequently. We would have a "friendly" discussion about American Firm—how we were the best, the toughest—and I never failed to mention the fact that if they didn't align with us, we'd take care of them. Our reputation preceded us, and many of them joined.

One particular group, the WAR Skins, didn't like how American Firm was constantly raining on their parade, getting noticed all the time, stealing recruits, and cutting into their territory. WAR Skins had grown big at one time in the Inland Empire of Southern California. We were the only threat to them. I was working diligently on recruitment and was much more successful than they were in bringing new people into their group. In addition to more members, we were creating strong alliances, which were really putting a squeeze on the WAR Skins. All around them, groups of Skins were dropping their name and taking ours until the WAR Skins had only Riverside and Rubidoux.

I'm sure that particular group of Skins was sick to death of hearing my name all over the place. Apparently they thought if they could get rid of me, they would have a chance to reclaim their name and their losses. Everything else would fall into place.

I had been dating a girl named Heather off and on since I was eighteen. She was a couple of years younger than me, and I had gotten her involved in the whole Skinhead Movement. I treated Heather the way a lot of Skins treated their girlfriends. Within the Movement, there was a certain amount of respect you showed to women, although it wasn't very high. It had to do with making babies and ensuring that the white race continued through these Aryan women, and that was about it. Machismo, control, and order were on a higher list of priorities than respecting girls. With Heather in particular, I maintained an "I don't want her—you can't have her" mentality. As soon as she would start dating someone else, I would tell her I wanted her back and she'd break up with that person. I'd be with her for a short while, and then I would feel like I'd had enough and break up with her again. This happened several times. One day, after we had broken up for a while, she called me.

"Mike wants to talk to you," she said. Her voice was strangely void of all emotion. I knew Mike was involved with the WAR Skins, and I figured this couldn't be good news for me.

"No, I don't want to," I said. Heather tried a little harder. I could almost see Mike on the other side of the line, urging her on.

"Well," she added, "why don't you come and meet me at Denny's?" The restaurant she was referring to was in WAR Skins' territory, and there was no way I was going in there to be set up.

"No. When you come back to town, we'll talk." I hung up, knowing that she wouldn't call me for a while, perhaps even worried for her own life. While I wasn't happy with what she had been half-heartedly trying to set me up for, I couldn't really blame her. Survival was survival.

In the meantime, I had many of the same goals as my Aryan brothers and began to write additional articles for the Aryan magazines. I even began working to de-escalate wars between the Skinheads so we would become stronger. I knew that if we were united, no racial gang or platoon of cops could be strong enough to bring us down.

Interestingly enough, it soon became apparent that white power leadership weren't the only people noticing my influence and leadership abilities. The Redlands Police Department and San Bernardino County sheriff's deputies had been tailing me. Over the next few months, my world would grow increasingly hot.

Despite being tailed frequently by the cops, I liked being the man with the power. There were a lot of perks, and life seemed pretty good. It certainly was never boring. Plus, if anybody messed with me or someone that I was close to, they would have to answer for it. Everyone knew it. Most people didn't try me.

My brothers didn't know much about my gang affiliations, but they did know that if they ever had a problem they could come to me to solve it. One night at a party, Mat and Phil both had way too much to drink. Phil left the party, but Mat passed out on the couch. Two clowns poured bleach on his hair while he slept. When Mat woke up, the caustic bleach streamed into his eyes and caused him incredible pain. His eyes turned solid red and looked horrible. We rushed him to a hospital, and he had to take some special medicine for several days in a row. The doctor said he could have gone blind. Man, I was pissed and ready to commit homicide. Less than two weeks later I had a chance for vengeance.

"Hey," said Phil. "There's going to be a party. Those two idiots are supposed to be there." He told me he'd found out which one was specifically responsible for hurting Mat's eyes.

I wasn't about to let anyone get away with causing my brother pain. Phil and I and a couple of my friends went to the party. We drove my white VW Bug, a 1972 Super Beetle, up to a rest area on highway 330. It was halfway up toward Forest Falls, on a turnout near a creek and a grassy area that commuters and cops couldn't see from the road. Out in the middle of nowhere, this was a popular place for underage kids to party.

In advance, we had decided how Phil could finger the right guy. After being there for only a few minutes, Phil put his hand on one guy's shoulder—some Gothic kid. I studied him. He was insignificant to me except for the fact that I was about to pound his head into the dirt. It was the unmistakable sign, and as soon as the kid was fingered, I bum-rushed him.

"This is for my brother Mat!" I yelled. Some guy pulled me off, and my buddy grabbed him, allowing me to get at the Goth kid again, and then someone else pulled me off him once more.

"You had better leave this place now!" I said, my eyes blazing with hatred. I was trying to twist out of the grasp of so many people holding me back. "If I ever catch you at a party that Mat or Phil or I go to, you'd better get the hell out of there, or I will kill you!" Apparently, he believed me and never showed up at a party they were at or left immediately whenever they arrived. It's a good thing Mat didn't go blind, or I probably would have killed this guy. That kind of force and intimidation came so easily to me now as a gang leader. I liked knowing I could "take care" of whatever problems my brothers had. I liked having that kind of power and influence. Now the only problem was the local law enforcement getting in my way.

THE HEAT OF THE LIMELIGHT

Even before my mother's conversation with the RP officer, it seemed like police and sheriff deputies were everywhere I went. I had to carefully stash my weapons, watch my drinking and driving, and avoid my usual hangouts. This was not an easy task for me. In working at the docks, I made a lot of money. I was a very popular man because I always had a lot of cash and power, and I attracted lots of girls. Everything, it seemed, would have been perfect—if it wasn't for the surveillance.

One night I had gotten away with an American Firm brother. We were traveling through the Inland Empire on the way to a party when we stopped at a mom and pop service station to go to the bathroom. Some Hispanics were hanging out, and they watched us as we entered the store. We ignored them, but they must've been thinking, *Two little white boys will make a good target.* They figured we were the way to score quick and make their getaway.

As soon as we stepped foot out of the mini-mart doors, they started talking battle language. The scene escalated amazingly fast, and it was looking frightening for my friend and I, who were seriously outnumbered. Two or three ganged up on each of us, and we were getting severely beaten. It was the first time I'd been beaten so badly in a long time. I found myself wondering if either one of us was going to make it out alive.

By chance, I was able to get into my pocket, grab my knife, and stick the guy that was pummeling me the worst. He screamed loudly, and all his friends backed up a bit. Blood was spurting everywhere, and they decided to get out of there fast. As we watched the group peel out of the drive and take off, in shock I realized I was still holding the knife. We both looked at it and took off just as fast. Driving down the freeway, I chucked the knife out the window, far. No evidence is good evidence.

Violence in and around San Bernardino County continued to escalate and became more organized, so I was targeted as the man with material and leadership. I was tipped off that law enforcement had spent the last six months building a case against me. Pretty soon I was going to be cornered with no way out. Any way I analyzed it, it didn't look good. "Peace officers" were on my ass every day.

One evening I looked out the window. An unmarked car was parked across the street. Sometimes they were marked, sometimes unmarked, but they knew that *I* knew they were there. Every time I walked out of my house, they were practically camped out on my doorstep. I was constantly being pulled over, searched, and checked. I had stuff in my car that I didn't want them to see. I couldn't ask any of my friends to come get me because they'd be searched too, and I didn't want anyone fingered or involved in more trouble than we were in already. I decided to walk a few blocks to our hangout spot and see if I could lose the tail. With dismay, I tucked my 9mm into my drawer and turned away. I felt naked and unprotected without it. A lot of people would have wanted to know I didn't have a gun on me; I would have made a great target.

Later that evening, I was walking on Redlands Boulevard downtown, headed toward Vince's house. I was wearing my wife beater and was "totally yoked." (This was our term to mean I had been "pushing" weights. Totally yoked meant we were buffed, big, ripped.) In addition, my ink was showing on my arms and my braces were down—a sure sign of an impending fight or that I was in a crappy mood and would mess with anyone I came into contact with. A Redlands PD patrol car passed me going in the opposite direction. As he passed, I got the feeling he was checking me out solidly and would be coming back around. When he had passed a good ten to fifteen feet, I turned my head slightly to see that he was in the turning lane. I knew he was going to flip a U-turn and come back for me. Quickly, I crossed the street, swallowing my panic with the intention of hopping the fence by the church, hoping to make it to the building before they could stop me. However, the light stayed green for them and they pulled over in front of me and both got out. There were two officers, a trainer and a rookie. There was nowhere to go. I knew better than to run from them.

"Hey, come over here," said the trainer. "Put your hands on the hood."

I let them pat me down, and that's when they found the buck knife I had in my back pocket. They threw it on the hood of the car, continuing their search.

"What's going on?" they asked, knowing I wouldn't tell them. "What's your name?" they asked, even though they already knew who I was. They were hoping to catch me in a lie, catch me at something. "Where are you headed? What's going to happen?" I told them who I was and that I was just headed to the mall to do a little shopping.

"Yeah, right," the older one sniggered. "We're going to take pictures of your tatts."

"Fine, whatever," I said resignedly. "You guys already have all this stuff about me on file."

"That's okay," he said. "We'll just get it all from you again." He and the other cop started taking pictures of the tattoos on my arms. They were taking their own sweet time.

"I'm keeping your knife because it's too long," said the trainer. "Technically, I could run you in. I won't do it this time, but you better believe next time I will."

Right, I thought. *I've heard that one a hundred thousand times before.* I just nodded and looked away.

"We're keeping an eye on you, TJ," he said. They both stared at me, hard. "You'd better watch your back."

I could tell they were disappointed I wasn't packing. They were trying to catch me with something—dying to get something on me that would stick. Wanting to laugh at what idiots they were, I was nervous about the tip I had gotten that they were also investigating my involvement in a couple of assault cases. I had good reason to feel anxious as I walked away, and decided I'd better stop at the mall for a few minutes at least.

Day after day, life continued on like this for about six months. I become acquainted with several of these officers on a first-name basis. They certainly knew all my body parts well after so many searches. I got hit with a nightstick once—just once. *Rodney King must've been on something good*, I thought. It hurt like hell. The violence didn't scare me. I'd been beat up enough by other Skins to know I would get over it, but I certainly didn't invite more of it. I tried to create a friendly relationship with as many of the officers as I could. Of course we didn't ever trust each other, but violence was less likely to erupt. Some of them seemed to feel the same way. Others were immovable and determined to hate my guts and throw me in the slammer.

Dale Jensen, a detective from the San Bernardino Sheriff's Department, had me on his list. He was about my size and very stocky. Dale is what I would call a no-nonsense officer: he was blunt, up front, and didn't bullshit with me. He simply told it like it was. I came to appreciate his candor. At the time, he labeled me as "definitely a person of interest." Later, Dale made a remark about this period of surveillance: "The fact that TJ was very, very intelligent made him even more dangerous than your average gang member. Seriously, if we could have found a way to put TJ in jail, we would have because of his political views . . . We were much more interested in him than any of his underlings, and we were gathering as much intelligence on him as we could to build a case that would put him away for a long, long time. The problem was TJ's influence over the youngsters. He helped make the problem in the community much bigger than we wanted it to be. His influence was too widespread."

I wasn't worried about going to prison; I knew I could handle it in there as well as I handled the streets. American Firm had some connections to prison gangs, especially Aryan Brotherhood (AB), or the Brand as it is known, and I came to realize that I had as much of what it took to be a leader inside stone walls and steel as well as I did on the outside. As long as they didn't force me to be a dope dealer, I would have survived. In fact, I would have likely become a leader in prison as well because that ensured survival, and I liked being alive. A lot of Skins eventually became AB after a while. It was *the* brand for white supremacists in prison. They pushed everything—drugs, prostitution, distortion, protection. I would have likely become involved in it all, whether I wanted to or not.

While the threat of a prison experience didn't frighten me, I still didn't want to lose my freedom—and I certainly didn't want to spend any time in there. In prison, at least they segregated people according to their crime. Jail was another story. I had spent time in jail and I was uncomfortable with knowing that in jail I could be stuck with a murderer or rapist or someone convicted of sodomy—everyone is all trapped and wedged in together. By this time, I had buddies in and out of jail all the time, and a few close associates on their way to prison or already in prison. My cousin Gilbert was serving time for armed robbery. Many of my Skin brothers considered prison a badge of honor. If imprisoned, they became POWs (prisoners of war) in the battle for the Movement.

As I thought about it, I realized that my real fear was not prison but having my gun rights taken from me. It was very important to me to own and carry a firearm. Since these weapons were a daily part of my protective gear, I was already feeling open and exposed under surveillance. If I were to get booked with a felony, police could come into my house anytime they wanted. They could mandate to me who I could associate with and who not to. I made up my mind. It was time for me to look to another avenue—any other avenue. I had to get out, and fast. But where would I go? How?

I was looking for options of escape and found one that would actually *pay* me to go away for a while. I joined the United States Marine Corps. It seemed like a fairly cool deal, and I had the hope that in my absence the cops might simply cool it. Going into the Marines actually saved me from several huge messes. The most obvious was the case the cops were building against me. The second was another DUI charge.

As I was preparing for boot camp, I instinctively knew my life was about to change dramatically. I was anxious to hold on tight to my friends, and weirdly enough, my family. Feeling a little uneasy about this whole change of life, I borrowed my dad's truck without asking and went out partying. I got so drunk, I couldn't tell a road sign from a farmhouse and threw out the transmission. I made it close to home without killing anyone, but as I limped along in the truck, I was picked up by a California highway patrolman. Savvy as far as drunk drivers were concerned, he slapped the cuffs on me quickly. However, on the way down to spend time in the county jail on Third Street, I kept thanking my lucky stars it was HP and not a local sheriff deputy or RP that had picked me up. Surprisingly, the HP didn't access the local PD's or sheriff's databases, so he didn't ask me any questions about my tattoos or gang activities. My arrest solidified my resolve to get out of town, but now I didn't know if the DUI would keep me around long enough for the cops to nab me for something much more serious. It was getting too hot in my neighborhood.

8

The Few, the Proud, the Skinheads among the Marines

JUST BEFORE THE police were ready to bust me, I was whisked away by the U.S. military. I had signed up in Redlands at the Marine Corps recruitment office, in a little shopping center next to a cantina near the Redlands Recreation Club. I did not have any felonies, which was the only thing they asked me. They didn't ask me if I was *about* to be busted with a felony or two. Joining the military got me out of California and away from the heat of law enforcement breathing down my neck. My recruiter even came to court with me and got me out of serving jail time for my DUI. The judge let it pass since I was joining the proud ranks of the Marines. I'm sure he thought, like my mother, that the service would straighten me out.

I chose the Marines because I felt they were the best of the best. Why not go all the way in my getaway? Surprisingly, it also provided an experience I actually enjoyed. On January 26, 1988, I entered Marine boot camp at the recruiting depot in San Diego. It was a little intimidating at first. Grown men were yelling in my face daily. To say it was a very, very intense environment is a direct understatement, but I had grown to love intensity, and this was nothing new. Aside from the fact that *I* was now used to being the one doing the yelling, I loved it. I lay exhausted in my bunk at nights, realizing it was probably one of the best experiences and opportunities that had ever happened in my life. Like my experience with the Skins, I had found a place that felt like home.

Thriving in boot camp gave me my first real sense of accomplishment. In addition to that, as a Marine I earned my diploma. That was a big deal for me since I had dropped out of high school. It boosted my confidence. I was starting to actually believe in myself. Certainly there were many days of sheer hell in boot camp, yet when I graduated I felt ten thousand feet high! My family was cheering for me in the stands. I began to think of possibilities beyond life with the Skins.

This was the first time in my life that I began to feel valued for who I was. For once, it wasn't the money I made or the violence I could create, the girls I could attract, the alcohol I could buy, or the people I could recruit. I began to slightly broaden my perspectives. In fact, my first time out on leave, I didn't even want to hang out with my former associates. The only friend I went to see when I came home was my old girlfriend Heather. She was the first Skinhead girl I had ever dated and had remained one of my closest friends.

Unfortunately, wanting to disentangle myself from the Movement did not last long. I was sent to a nine-to-five job at Kaneohe Marine Corps in Hawaii. I was a 7011, meaning that my MOS, or Marine Occupational Service, was aircraft recovery. The job I was going to do in the corps was in aircraft recovery, and we were to build land-based runways for combat situations. Of course, since we weren't involved in any active combat at that time in that area, it was an easy, laid-back career.

While many people might love a soft job like that, my challenge was taken from me. All the joy, passion, and drive I had experienced so far in the corps was sucked right out of me. I was supposed to be in paradise—on the windward side of the island of Oahu, so lush and scenic it was breathtaking—but I just didn't enjoy it. Within days, it was a mental, emotional, and physical struggle just to get out of bed and go to work.

I found myself wishing administration had put me in the grunt corps, always on the go, doing the real physical stuff I loved. In the grunt corps I could have excelled. As it was, I was given enormous amounts of free time to hang out at clubs and beaches with girls on vacation (which gets old faster than you think). I often had nothing better to do than get wasted and get into fights. In MOS school in New Jersey, I had already been arrested for two alcohol-related offenses. On the Island of Oahu, I was drinking even more heavily. In short, it was the worst place the Marines could have sent me.

On base I got along with some of my commanding officers, but there were a few of the sergeants and some corporals who were absolute jerks. Certain "lifers" spent their entire day bad-talking the organization, which pissed me off. They also liked to make life suck for the lower ranks and made it sound like I would never move up, move sideways, or do anything to change things for the better. I felt stuck again. I had no power and apparently no way to gain power in a positive way. That's when I began to pursue that which had made me feel powerful in the past.

Within only weeks after arriving in Hawaii, I started contacting former friends and got back into the Movement. Being sick of the Marines escalated my desire and involvement in racist activities. Knowing that I had had an effect on the Movement whenever I had been involved made me feel powerful, and I wanted to feel like my life was under my control again. Upland Dave told me that due to my articles in *WAR* and other racist publications, shortly after I left for the Marine Corps, Tom Metzger—*the* Tom Metzger, publisher of *WAR* newspaper—had invited several of my associates to come down to Fallbrook, California, to talk with him. I was excited for them, and more than just a little jealous that they would have this inside track. I poured that energy into my renewed commitment to the Movement in Hawaii.

During my free time, I continued my self-indoctrination. My room on the third floor of the barracks was known for loud white power music, heavy drinking, partying, and Nazi swastikas. I handed out books like *The Turner Diaries, Mein Kampf,* and more. I began ordering and handing out all kinds of Aryan propaganda to most of my friends and associates. Unbeknownst to me—although not surprising—at this same time, Timothy McVeigh was passing out *The Turner Diaries* and related materials in *another* one of the United States's armed forces. Everyone, from roommates to commanding officers, knew what I was doing in my barracks. They turned a blind eye and allowed me to keep it up or joined me in it.

I was disappointed to learn from Upland Dave and other associates that after I left, the Skins began swiftly declining in numbers. At get-togethers and parties where previously a hundred or more Skins would show, they were lucky to see twenty. American Firm and American Front were both losing members rapidly and no one seemed to know what to do about it. Toward the latter months of 1988, a Hammerskin chapter was organized in Hollister, Northern California. Using the name CHS, or California Hammerskins, this chapter originated from a meeting between WAR Skins and Holland when they met on the set of *Oprah*, in Chicago. Hammerskins was becoming a national craze, and Holland was the first in California to latch onto the concept.

From a distance, I heard rumors of major changes but couldn't do anything about any of them. I hated being locked up in this place so far from home. I was drinking huge amounts of alcohol and proceeded to get busted three more times for alcohol-related incidents. One was an assault I committed in Waikiki against some tourist who ticked me off. That charge was later reduced to disorderly conduct. I received another charge for public intoxication when I got into a shouting match with a policeman on the street, and a third DUI, when I was so drunk I heisted some guy's car and didn't even realize what I had done. What I did realize was that I had to do something with all my extra energy before I went crazy or killed someone. I started recruiting friends and creating fellow believers in racist philosophies. Even though I didn't have an official okay from Upland Dave, I didn't care. I spent the majority of my time in that initiative.

As before, I was always on the lookout for more effective ways to build my skills. One valuable ability the Marines taught me was how to be a much better recruiter for the Skins. The basis for this was what I learned in boot camp: the military technique of "tear down and rebuild." Essentially, it's a very slow and steady way to change a person's outlook on life, self-perceptions, and loyalties. It's been used for thousands of years in military settings and has been honed to an incredibly effective method of control. The first step is demoralizing a recruit's way of thinking, shattering it into tiny pieces, then rebuilding it with new thoughts and belief systems. The Marine Corps does that to everybody. It certainly worked on my psyche. As a naive young man in camp, I sucked it all in. I embodied the Marines and by the time I graduated, they could have sent me out to battle, told me I could take a bullet, and I would've done it. Proudly, in fact.

I began experimenting with some of these Marine recruiting techniques in Hawaii. I really didn't care when I made mistakes over there: only a few people saw me being an idiot. I could handle that. At first, I made some really dumb errors, like being far too aggressive, akin to putting a swastika in their hand the second day in. I learned to cultivate the individual instead of trying to harvest them too quickly.

There was a woman on base who had the perfect Skinhead girl haircut; she was prime for recruitment. She was always hanging out with one guy in particular. I started to get friendly with both of them, and we began to party together a bit. I felt confident I could get her in, and once I did, her friend would join as well. They were beginning to like the music and, little by little, had started to teeter in our direction. However, one night a group of us were drinking heavily and preparing to "take care of business" with some Samoans who had been talking trash on the other side of the island. So much booze was flowing that the established members were spouting obscene, white power, racist remarks and definitely using hard-core battle language.

The girl and her friend stayed for a bit but then made excuses to leave.

"Naw, stay!" I said. "Come and party some more!"

"We're going to go," she said. "Things are getting a little too crazy." I knew we had totally blown it when they were always "too busy" to hang out or party anymore. Lesson: Only some recruits come in hard-core. Keep established people and recruits apart until it's obvious that the recruits are ready for the next step.

Several months later, I had a further opportunity with a different girl and her boyfriend. This time I groomed them, ever so slowly. The girl was a military brat, about sixteen, who was hanging out on base. Her boyfriend was a Marine. We started by simply partying in my room in the barracks. After getting to know them better, a bunch of us went into town, including this couple, my friend William, and my girlfriend and I. We had stopped into a little restaurant to eat. William noticed some kind of commotion outside of the restaurant.

"Look out there, TJ," he said, and nodded through the window. There were a dozen or more Filipinos grouped together outside, staring menacingly at us. I'm sure it gave this girl and her boyfriend quite a fright. My brain started working quickly, but before I could react, one of their group came in and sat down across from us. By his confident looks and the way he held himself, I knew he was their leader.

"Are you white power?" he asked pointedly. There was no mistaking the derision in his voice—or the challenge.

"Sure!" I said, before anyone could speak. "Sure we are!" He was a little taken aback. I think even the group was shocked at my boldness. They probably thought we were about to get killed.

"Well . . . we don't want you or your white power around here," he said, shifting back into his machismo.

"Look," I countered. "Are you, or are you not, proud of being Filipino?"

"Well, yes," he said, beginning to look uncomfortable again. "Of course I am."

"Well, you *should* be," I answered. "You're Filipino and it's important to be proud of your heritage. We're proud of being white. It's where we come from. We're proud of our race, our culture, and our heritage. That's all white power is. You're proud of being Filipino, and we're proud of being white. It's that simple." He didn't know what to say. I had turned the tables on him. Ignoring him, I went back to eating, and the conflict was over. He and his gang walked away.

This confrontation, from the initial fear to the way it was handled, probably helped to solidify this young couple into our group. Two days later, during another one of my parties, we gave her a Skinhead girl haircut, and the guy shaved his head. That was recruiting at its finest.

I had started writing again for Aryan publications. I wrote under the title USMC (United Skins in Military Clothes) about how Affirmative Action was being used in the military for all the wrong reasons. I described how good, deserving white men were not being raised in ranks, and even deserving Hispanics were getting passed over for women and blacks. All the hatred I was beginning to feel for the Marines gushed out into the pages, feeding more distrust for government and military.

CHANGING OF THE GUARD

My next leave was for thirty days in July and August of 1989. This time I didn't call Heather. I had big plans. I arrived at a massive American Firm party at a house in Chino, in cooperation with the Chino Hills Skins (CHS). The house belonged to a red-headed CHS, a leader who went by the name of Blaze. He lived in a huge, old Victorian fixer-upper on two and a half acres. There must have been 200–250 people partying in the house and on the grounds, listening to live bands and drinking heavily. We had an alliance with Blaze's gang and we were all good friends.

There were a lot of people in the house—including perhaps a hundred new Skins who didn't know who I was. I certainly hadn't seen most of them around, and I didn't feel like I had been gone that long.

"Who the hell are all these people?" I asked Upland Dave on the way in. "You told me you were declining in numbers!"

"Ah, man, we were. We like to call these guys Geraldo Skins!" he said, laughing.

"*Geraldo Skins?*" I asked quizzically. "What the freak are you talking about?" He laughed even harder at my naivety on this subject.

"You've been in Hawaii for too long. Didn't you see that show on

Geraldo where that Skin broke Geraldo's nose?" he asked me. *Oh, yeah. Everyone had seen that one.* The media and television stations capitalized on the event, making sure that 99 percent of America saw the group of quarreling, extremely violent Skinheads get into an argument that erupted into a fistfight, right in the studio. A kid smashed a chair and ended up breaking Geraldo's nose. Of course Geraldo didn't seem to mind showing the sequence of him clutching at his broken and bleeding nose hundreds of times over the next several days. It boosted his ratings incredibly high. He made a great victim.

"Yeah, well," my friend went on. "That created this"—he motioned around the room at the huge number of green Skins—"so every kid who hated Geraldo and didn't know what he wanted to be when he grew up said, 'I want to be a SKIN!' We've literally been picking up these guys left and right." *Way to go, Geraldo.*

I walked further into the room, amazed but really happy. Searching among the crowd for any other familiar face besides Dave's, I finally caught the eye of a bunch of people sitting in the kitchen. Apparently it was the leadership table, and a great roar rose up when they saw me. I felt hundreds of eyes on me as I sauntered across the room to boisterous greetings from Blaze and Lance from Chino Hills, along with Ace, Gabriel, and a couple other of my Skin affiliation leaders. I started bullshitting with them as though I'd never been gone.

"You're lookin' good, TJ!" they all bellowed. I just grinned. I was even more heavily yoked than before I left, thanks to the Marines.

"Who the freaking hell is this dude?" I heard several people gasp and whisper. I knew they had to be wondering, since no one who wasn't someone could just walk up and sit at *that* table.

"That's TJ Leyden," was the reply that rippled through the crowd from one or two older Skins, and everyone shut up. The Skin leadership and I had a great deal to discuss as we drank through the night. The Movement had been faltering for a bit, and now leadership was facing considerable problems. Just as the numbers had dwindled abysmally, the sudden increase in members, power, and new alliances was creating huge rifts and the biggest outbreak of violence ever experienced during the Skinhead Wars.

For one thing, American Firm had aligned with Chino Hills Skins as well as the South Bay Skins, while American Front aligned with WAR Skins and NorthSide Firm. The LADS (LA Death Squads) hadn't officially aligned with anyone, choosing instead to bounce back and forth between white power and the Cholos, a dominant Hispanic group. The balance of power was shifting, creating a vacuum within lines of authority and coalitions between groups.

As the night progressed, I could tell I certainly didn't have all the answers. Something else was taking place behind the scenes. I didn't know what it was, but I could feel the undercurrent. There was subtle body language and occasional vague comments accompanied by a wink or a nod. I took Dave aside quietly.

"What the hell is going on?" I asked him.

"I can't talk about it yet, TJ," he said, shuffling from one foot to the other uncomfortably.

"Why?"

"I'll tell you as soon as I can," he said, his eyes serious. "I swear it!"

What could I say? My hands were tied. He was the official leader, and I certainly couldn't do anything about it, stationed half a world away. My power was obviously limited. I did, however, discover that I had work to do that could maintain my rank and some modicum of respect of the people while enduring my time in the military. While I was on leave, I would be referred to as the Enforcer. I could drink to that, and I did.

One of the problems American Firm was having in Upland was a Skin in the ranks who had recently "gotten out of line," apparently running his mouth and talking trash about the leadership. I made a phone call.

"You need to watch your back," I said menacingly. "You need to be very, very careful what you say." He was belligerent and a smart-ass, as I expected him to be. A few nights later, when he was feeling fairly safe again, I went to a park I knew was his local hangout. Upland Dave and Paul got out of the car with me, and we approached this newer group of Skins. We were all wearing our black Docs with white laces, black Levis, and black, American Firm sweatshirts with IE Chapter emblazed on them. We were dressed like their friends.

The guys all greeted us, but I strode straight up to the kid I knew I was looking for and cold-cocked him. I hit him so hard, I thought I heard something crack just before he went down like a sack of potatoes. My buddies laughed, but the other Skins there were in complete shock. I doubt they would have jumped me, even if Dave and Paul weren't there.

"This is what you get when you start running your freakin' mouth and being a smart-ass," I snarled. "Respect your elders. Respect your

leaders, and keep your mouth shut, or you'll get much worse than this."
I gestured down to the crumpled body. "I guarantee you that!"

I had no problem being an enforcer. I actually thought it was fun. My
favorite part was to see other people's reactions when they found out who
I was. Rumors were spreading fast.

On one of these jobs, if I had the possibility of getting jumped, then
I would bring somebody with me. If simple "justice" needed to be served
against a rival gang or rival Skins, I would usually go alone. Coldly, quietly, and unbeknownst to California police, I enforced whatever leadership asked of me. After visiting my family for the first couple of days, I
was at the disposal of my Skin brothers. If they had a target—anyone
that needed to be taught a lesson—I was the guy to do it. It was a way of
protecting the leadership and keeping us all out of trouble. After all, by
the time an investigation from the authorities took place, I would be long
gone. Who would suspect a Marine in a drive-by? Or suspect a Marine on
an assault on a gang leader in a Hispanic neighborhood?

Upland Dave took me to a tattoo parlor for a "gift." Though I wasn't
entirely sure why, I had two crossed hammers tattooed on my body. All
I knew was that I was in the middle of a shifting and changing environment. It was exciting to me. I longed to be home for good.

Back in Hawaii, I continued my recruiting in the corps. I had a lot of
free reign in my room in the barracks on base. It was the size of a studio
apartment, with cinderblock walls all the way around. Still, it was pretty
nice. There were supposed to be three of us in one area. However, one of
my roommates was a drug dealer, so he was never there. Another roommate was always in town with his girlfriend. In addition, whenever there
were new recruits, those in authority made it a point *not* to give me a black
or Hispanic roommate.

I didn't care that I was openly racist now, and not too many other
people did, either. The folks that generally gave me the most crap about
my racism were whites. I hated these race traitors because I felt like they
just didn't get it. Even around blacks and Hispanics I didn't keep my
mouth shut, and I nearly got into an altercation with a black Marine that
could have gotten really ugly.

In response to a fight I had gotten into, I was on barracks restriction,
though it really didn't mean much. I had to go down every hour and sign
in, so they could tell I was present. I had been showing up every time to
sign in, but late in the night I got lazy and was the last one to be marked

in. The black guy on guard duty started giving me a lot of crap. He knew I was openly racist and on that particular day, he seemed bound and determined to punish me for it.

"Look, I'm here," I said. "Can you just sign it so I can go?"

"Screw you!" he barked at me. "No, I'm not going to sign it, you Nazi Skinhead!"

"Dude, you know what?" I said, on the verge of taking him down right there. "You're way out of line and I'm going to—"

The black sergeant came over, walking quickly.

"What's up?" he asked, his eyes looking carefully at both of us, our muscles tensed and waiting.

"This guy won't sign the roster that I'm here," I complained.

The sergeant came over and signed the column for me so I could go.

"What the freak are you doing?" cried the guy on guard duty. They knew each other because they were both cooks on the wing side.

"He's one of us," the sergeant said bluntly, gesturing to me. "He believes in separatism." The other man stared hard at him, then at me, his mind furiously processing this new information. Like Black Nationalists and other separatist leaders in the seventies and eighties, we were simultaneously promoting a new order. After an agreement was established between many of the groups in 1984, we all began working together to establish an America where people would be fully separated into groups: Atzland, or Hispanic America; the New Mecca for blacks; the White American Bastian for the Aryan whites; and Northern Cuba for other Hispanics and Latinos.

"Yeah, well," said the guard, his voice filled with venom, "when the shit hits the fan, they're going to blame the black man. They're going to stab you in the back."

"No, *he* won't," said the sergeant pointedly. "He will stab you in the *chest*. He'll look you right in your face and tells you he hates you. It's these other dogs who pretend to be nice and always tell jokes behind your back that cannot be trusted." He squared his shoulders and looked his comrade full in the face. "Don't ever NOT do your duty again," he said quietly, but with great intensity, "or I'll turn you in."

I knew this sergeant well. I saw him reading books from "Master Fard" Muhammad, Elijah Muhammad, Minister Louis Farrakhan, and even Khalid Abdul Muhammad. He was always reading things just as salacious, racist, separatist, and violent as what I was reading.

Sometimes we would discuss certain materials. He saw me reading the *WAR* newspaper, and we discussed *The Final Call*, which is the nation of Islam's paper. When we saw each other, we would say, "Hey, what's up!" and "Asalaamo Alaikum." That meant "peace be unto you." I found it friendly and ironic, since we both believed in the separation and eventual death of all other races but our own. Our respect for each other was based on a twisted commonality. We were Marines for the government, but underneath, we were soldiers for our Movements to divide America.

A few months later, back in the States, my friend Jeremy Reinnman was shot in Van Nuys, California, by rival Hispanic gang members employed by Lucky's Supermarket. Others were seriously injured that night as well. Ashley Brown had been shot in the back and one of his lungs had collapsed. In addition, they sliced him with a box cutter from his lip almost to his ear. Things took a grim turn. If white power hadn't played it serious before, now everything they did was for keeps. Jeremy Reinnman became famous for being paralyzed and in a wheel chair. He was Tom Metzgar's new poster boy. Tom put him on the cover of *WAR* and used him to get a huge amount of publicity and interest in white power. He also got lawyers for Jeremy and other legal advice. I was glad someone was doing something. I wanted to go back to the States and blow somebody's head off. Somebody needed to get paid back. This was war.

One of the highlights of my stay in Hawaii was when my brother Phil came to visit. He hadn't seen me in a while because of his own military adventures. When he got off the plane that early afternoon, he was looking bigger and more muscular than I had ever seen him. I could tell he was happy to see me, and I was certainly happy to see him. Phil was the first one to visit me, and we did some of the usual tourist stuff—Diamond Head and the North Shore to watch the big waves and the girls. We went out partying a lot, as well as all the partying in my barracks. He thought this lifestyle was pretty fun, although I could tell he was shocked at how entrenched I was in the Movement. It was part of my every waking hour. I even left him alone at a bar one night to put some loudmouth in check. In Hawaii it was a little different because I didn't have a widespread name or reputation yet. It was taking a while, but slowly I was establishing a pecking order and the respect that I was seeking.

Phil shared how he had hurt his knee on the Slide for Life during Phase II of boot camp and was sent home. This was devastating for him. Just a few months earlier, our little brother Mat had made it through and was shipped to Guantanamo Bay. Phil and I spent a lot of time talking about the corps, and during his stay he spoke to many of the guys in my unit. By the time he headed for home, he had decided to give the military a second try. He didn't know, but I could tell he would end up with great success and even a meritorious promotion.

When Phil left, I got the feeling he was worried for me. I know he went home and tried to open my mother's eyes to the knowledge I had gotten worse instead of better. I think a lot of moms think the military—especially the Marines—will straighten their boys up. What they don't realize is that the military is simply a microcosm of society. Whatever problems manifest in society will also manifest within the military, at least to some degree. He told my family that they had lost me to the White Power Movement—that I was gone for good. My mom wouldn't believe it. She was the queen of total denial.

Upland Dave had been true to his word and kept me informed about the dramatically changing climate of the Movement at home. The crossed hammers tattoo Dave had given me during my leave was to represent the newly formed Western Hammerskins, representing my allegiance to a changing order back home. Much of American Firm, American Front, and WAR Skins had collapsed to the point that there was no real organization left in the Skins. However, Ashley Brown from American Front, Dave VanVooris from American Firm, and Paul Smith from Fourth Reich went to a concert in Oklahoma City and met the Confederate Hammerskins. Holland's group had failed, but these guys decided to start a functioning Western Hammerskins group in Southern California.

A flopped Aryan concert had changed the political scene even more and had brought factions into sharp focus, especially as people like Tom Metzgar and others had gotten involved. Publicity had raised awareness of white power in a dramatic way, and people either hated us or loved us. Major uprisings were taking place in Hammerskin Nation chapters throughout the country, especially in the south. Texas had been hit hard with hate crimes, and law enforcement was hitting back. Most Confederate Hammerskins were caught and jailed for a number of crimes.

Despite the ongoing turmoil at home, I continued to feel completely supported by my Aryan beliefs. I began to focus on bringing more people into the Movement—especially now that we were becoming united in groups all over the nation. To me it was exciting. I didn't know how to shut up about it. I didn't really need to. Only one time during my stint in the Marines was I reprimanded for all the hate material in my personal space.

"Put your shit away!" Sergeant Kenny yelled at me, as he looked around at all my racist paraphernalia. I did exactly what he said while he was in the room. Then as soon as he left, I got it all back out again: the posters, the wall hangings, the hate music . . . the works.

I also got more tattoos at this point, and the military didn't care. Shortly after returning from my next leave, I went crazy with inking my body. I had a Celtic cross and an Aryan fist, with S-K-I-N and H-E-A-D down the back of my arms that people saw every day. I finally got a set of bolts on my back for the stabbing that had erupted before boot camp.

Although I had covered up a large swastika on my leg when I first went into the service, I now boldly tattooed two SS-bolts on my neck, two full inches above my collar. These bolts were also earned for stabbing a kid who was at the wrong place at the wrong time while I was on leave. I never caught any flack about those very visible bolts until a gunny from another division made me wear bandages on my neck during the day. They didn't care what I did in my barracks at night or who saw me off base in my marine haircut and T-shirt with the bolts proudly displayed. I was a walking advertisement for hate in the U.S. military.

LOOKING FOR LOVE . . . IN ARYAN FACES

It was tough to be a racist in Hawaii. It was easy to hold onto my beliefs, but it was certainly tough to be happy. Except for girls on vacation, most of the women were Polynesian. Being dead-set on my goals in the White Power Movement, I didn't want anything to do with anyone except a Skinhead girl. I had seen too many good racists get twisted around because of a non-Aryan girl. I wouldn't give anyone else the time of day.

I started writing girls back home in the States who were sympathetic to the cause. One girl, Nicole Rodman, caught my interest. Her best friend, Babs, was married to Dave VanVooris. Dave was one of my closest friends and was the one that got me connected to the American Firm when we were younger. He told Nicole about me and she sent the first letter. We began corresponding back and forth for six months before I got out of the military. She intrigued me, and I always looked forward to her letters.

Nicole had originally gotten involved in white power through white friends and associates she had met. It was understandable. She was brought up very poor and was raised in some of the worst barrios of LA.

"Every day I went to school," she told me, "I was accosted. Drunks in the street, potheads at school, and freakin' aliens were always trying to touch me or rob me." She resented having to take their crap and couldn't wait to get out of there. All of those experiences solidified white power in her mind. Now she was living in Texas, in a house with a bunch of other Skinheads. She really liked it, but things were starting to get strained there, and her letters reflected her frustration. Coming from a broken home and being on her own, she literally had nowhere to go.

By October of 1990, I couldn't take the Marines anymore. I set about to become discharged as quickly as possible, which would mean dishonorably. I tried to make alcohol a big enough issue to get me out. I was drinking as much as I weighed, and I was fighting whenever I could. I would fight in the E-Club, I would fight downtown, and I was often disorderly, even though this was what I thought being a Marine was all about.

It was frustrating to me that the administrators didn't have enough information to kick me out, so I gave them more. I revealed eight or nine incidents related primarily to alcohol that they had been totally unaware of. I told them about flunking out of alcohol school, getting busted down to Private, and several more incidents that were somehow not recorded in my files, including the big no-no: buying alcohol for Marines who were still minors.

When my first efforts to be discharged failed, I was shipped to Camp Pendleton. There I became involved in a major racial situation. This was not the first time for me. I learned that the military will never write the term *race riot* on any military reports or papers, as it attracts immediate, negative media attention that every branch of the military avoids at all costs. Unfortunately, this practice of covering up also kept the armed forces from ousting people like me. The situation came to a head when I threatened my administrators. I told the officer in charge point blank, "If you do not discharge me, I will create a media circus. I will bring out all of my racist behaviors and make life hell for you."

He could see I was serious. A week later, I was discharged from the service for "conduct unbecoming a Marine." Surprisingly, this involved only the numerous alcohol incidents and had nothing to do with my racism—or at least this is the excuse they used to avoid political fallout. Despite my tattoos and my consistently violent behavior, nothing was ever put in my records that had anything to do with being a racist. I really didn't care. I was just glad to go home and be in control of my own life again.

My mother drove down to pick me up at the airport. When I got off the plane, I thought she was going to faint. At first she was in shock at my appearance. How could I have come home from the military *more* entrenched in gang behavior, dress, and style than when I left? She was speechless, but only momentarily. Then she got angry.

"You promised me you'd never get a tattoo that can be seen!" she spat. I shrugged. It was too late—they were everywhere. I had many, many more tattoos than when I left for the service—twenty-two in fact—and I was particularly proud of the two SS lightning bolts so high on my neck that no shirt collar could hide them. These bolts scared people spitless, and I loved it. I had become militant and hard as stone, at least on the outside. I don't think my mother could stand to be in my presence. Her obvious disgust made me feel a little bit sick to my stomach, but I wasn't about to show it, especially because she wasn't alone.

My mother had brought a woman with her to pick me up at the airport. Nicole Rodman had left the Skinhead home in Texas and had come to meet me off the plane. My mother looked even more uncomfortable around her than she did me, but I was overjoyed. I felt as close to Nicole after six months of writing letters back and forth as I ever had to anyone. This new relationship was about to change my life in ways I would have never imagined.

9

ARYAN WARRIOR AND BRIDE
PREPARE FOR BATTLE

WHEN PHIL AND Mat first saw me as I arrived home, they both called me on the spot. One look at the SS bolts on my neck, they both said, "Uh, uh! No way."

"C'mon, TJ!" Mat added, protesting. It was the biggest shock for him because he hadn't seen me as recently as Phil had. "You can't live this way! Please have those bolts removed or covered. Please!"

"I like them," I said smugly. "It makes people run and hide; they're cool and intimidating." Phil stared at me.

"What are you planning to do for the rest of your life?" he asked. "Do you really think you're going to get anywhere with Nazi bolts on your neck like that?"

It was hard for me to admit, but they didn't work very well in the civilian world. I didn't have the money to remove them, but Phil had enough to have them modified. He took me down to have them covered with a skull with flames coming out. If you knew what you were looking for, you could still see the bolts underneath, but most people didn't. Whenever prospective employers or others asked why I had tattoos on my neck, I simply told them I had been a Marine. "Oh, okay," they would say, and then shrug. And that was that. Apparently, it was perfectly acceptable to have tatts as a former Marine. I could then continue to live my double life without question.

Two weeks after Nicole and I officially met in November of 1990, we were hanging out in the home of some new friends. Wally and Clarissa were members of Western Hammerskins. Upland Dave, Babs, Chris,

Jennifer, Amy, Wyatt, and a bunch of other Western Hammerskins and leaders had joined us. It was a fun gathering and the mood was light and festive. As we were talking, people asked Nicole how the two of us had met, and we shared how we had written each other for a while before our first meeting. The girls seemed to think this was romantic, and the talk turned to marriage.

"Hey, you two ought to have an Aryan wedding!" said Wyatt. He was a member of Hammerskin Nation and was one of the leaders in charge of WHS in California. Nicole and I looked at each. *Why not?* The impromptu Aryan wedding ceremony took place right there, at the house with Nazi and Confederate flags draped on the wall as our romantic backdrop. Wyatt performed the ceremony. Aryan weddings are not recognized officially by the state of California (unless Tom Metzgar or another ordained minister performed it), but people still did it all the time. For me, it didn't matter.

Nicole was wearing Levis, a Fred Perry shirt, and her Doc Martens, perfect wear for a Skinhead wedding. I was wearing Levis, my Docs, and a Ben Sherman shirt.

"I will be loyal to you," I said, looking at her. "I will honor you as my Aryan bride and I will use all my strength to protect you at all times." It was her turn.

"I pledge my undying loyalty and complete submission to you," she said. "I will honor, obey, respect, and follow your lead as the Aryan warrior of our family." Of course we didn't have rings to exchange at the time, but that didn't matter. I bought her an engagement ring for Christmas, and she gave me a charm that read, "My Aryan Warrior." Very quickly Nicole and I were caught up in the Movement in Southern California.

We lived for a little while at my mother's house. We kept to ourselves for the most part. One day my mom came into our room and saw that we had a large Nazi flag on the wall. Mom wouldn't put up with it for an instant.

"That comes down NOW!" she threatened. "Take it down or I will tear it down!"

It came down, but my inner walls of steel remained intact. So did Nicole's. She hated my mom, especially because my mother stood for everything Nicole didn't believe in. She thought my mother was weak, ignorant (for not supporting the Movement, and a race traitor for not even being a bit racist), and believed her polio had made her inferior.

Nicole believed my mother should have been marked for death. She didn't talk much about it, but there was ice between those two from the very beginning. It was the hardest on my mom, I think, for two reasons. First, my mother knew Nicole didn't have an ounce of respect for her. And second, she couldn't rectify in her mind that I truly wanted what I said I wanted—all the separatist mumbo-jumbo. Even deeper, she refused to believe I had a Hitler-like mentality.

"How can you love me and yet profess to hate those who are inferior?" she asked. "Look at me, TJ! Look at my polio! I'm diseased. I would be one of those that would have to be eliminated!" She looked at me with her imploring eyes and I didn't know what to say.

"I would always protect you," I mumbled awkwardly.

"No you wouldn't," she said adamantly. "You *couldn't*." I knew she was right. When it came to the war that we were all readying for, rallying for, my mother was a sure victim. I didn't want to look at her in that way. I put it out of my mind, but like a seething pit of snakes, it would raise its ugly head from time to time. Shortly after that it shocked me to find out that the man who invented the Polio vaccine—thereby saving my mother's life and countless others—was actually a Jew.

A NEW ORDER

Coming back from Oklahoma, Ashley, Dave and Paul created a growing chapter of Western Hammerskins. However, Ashley started going to college to be a lawyer, and Upland Dave wanted to go underground and become less vocal and less visible. He wanted me to go underground with him, but I said no. Paul didn't have the desire to continue once the other two were gone and he gave his authority to Wyatt. Jeremy Reinnman, who had gotten married at the Aryan Fest from his wheelchair, helped them to form a new group, but since Tom had made him famous and given him notoriety, he couldn't take any reigns. Jeremy was still an avid member, but he couldn't be in leadership because it could legally compromise his standing in the courts.

Although I had decided to join the WHS chapter of Hammerskin Nation while on leave from the Marine Corps, I was not fully made a member until late 1990. What pissed off Wyatt and some other local Skins is that I was validated and became a member of Hammerskin Nation by the national leaders, without having to be WHS. I made it known that I didn't want to work under the banner WHS. I was choosing to be in charge of regional recruiting for Hammerskin Nation instead of WHS. In other words, I didn't have to operate under anyone else. I was in control of how much power I had and how big I wanted to grow HN.

Personally, I wanted Hammerskin Nation to get large and strong and unite Skins from across the nation. I had experienced firsthand the chaos and violence of factions. I felt this was the answer to the Skinhead Wars and ugly turf debates when our real enemies, the Jews, blacks, Hispanics, and homosexuals, were outside of these factions. I knew I could make a difference. I planned to use all of my skills and energy to make it happen.

One thing I was particularly clear about was that a huge, successful Aryan Fest in California would bring in lots of new recruits to Western Hammerskins and let people know about our cause. People thought I was absolutely nuts.

"You gotta be kidding, TJ," said Upland Dave. "Aryan Woodstock in 1989 was so bad they called it Aryan Woodflop. There was so much political crap and media and stuff going on. People sat in the rain for three days, and no one was even allowed to play any music. Aside from the negotiating we did while we were there, that was the worst three days I've spent in my entire life!"

It was true that the Aryan concert had been a total failure. Tom Metzgar from *WAR* and "Nazi Bob" Heick, the originator of American Front, had tried to organize a concert of white power bands on a private farm near Napa, California. The land lease was a big joke. Heick and Metzger engaged in power struggles and poor planning throughout the process and had to go to court just to hold the event. Tom had been the former grand dragon of the Southern California Ku Klux Klan. He was very vocal about his beliefs, and people paid attention—too much attention. While Judge Snowden ruled that the gathering could take place, he ruled there could be no music—the main reason so many were coming. A few hundred people made it to the property before the landowner, Howard Londsale, succumbed to police pressure and allowed the authorities to close off the entrance. Stranded would-be attendees and hundreds of protestors spent a miserable weekend clashing in the rain over a concert that never took place.

I knew I had the ability to create something different. It would take planning, strategy, guts, and resources. I was on fire and got to work on the idea—much of it covertly.

In the meantime, I was writing as often as possible for different Aryan publications. Whenever we had something big go down, we wrote up an article and sent it in—anything we could do to get more people to take notice and join the Movement, especially our interpretation of it. I had been writing back and forth with some pretty powerful Movement leaders, including Tom Metzger. I realized that Tom had been paying attention to us for quite some time. His planning of the Aryan concert, Woodflop or not, actually acknowledged the fact that Skinheads had become a powerful force in the Movement, though notoriously volatile and dangerous. He had plans for soldiers like us, and he wanted to set about "taming" the Skins and making them a useful tool for the Movement.

In an interview for a local California station, Tom admitted to his scheme. "I'd tell the Skins grow your hair out," he said with a smile. "Change your clothes, grab a briefcase, and go to college . . . whatever you have to do to move up." Tom actually assisted more mature Skinheads to get their act together. That way they would be more powerful and could do more damage in a covert way.

I met Tom personally at a talk show called *Harvey and the Lion's Den*. A month later, I was in the audience of *Wally George*. Wally had been around the block many years, as the original father of talk shows, long before *Jerry Springer* and *Oprah*. Tom and Jeremy Reinnman were guests on his show. After the show, we went and partied at Jeremy's house in Torrance, California, and talked about what we could do to bring more people into the Movement. We talked about progression and advancement and what that looked like in our current situation in society.

"Don't worry about the blacks," Tom advocated. "Worry more about the government. The government is the enemy. The government is the problem." He looked at me and my friends. "Get ready," he said, his compelling eyes upon me. "Be prepared. Stuff is going to happen." I always had to laugh at Tom. Although we carried the same name, I always spoke my mind and he was incredibly good at being very vague. He had been around long enough that he would never cross that line—and while he couldn't be pinned down and cornered with evidence, everyone knew exactly where he was coming from and exactly what his message meant.

After that night, Tom invited me several times to drop by his home to pick up newspapers and propaganda to help spread the word of white power. I found out this wasn't Tom's original residence; it was a place he was renting since his own property had been seized in a civil lawsuit in 1990 and through another judgment in 1992. A few years before,

Tom had been linked with the murder of an Ethiopian man in Portland, Oregon. While he was never charged criminally, he was held responsible by a civil jury.

Still, the man sure wasn't living in a rat hole. I could tell he knew what he was doing. He had lost several million dollars, but it didn't matter. He continued his war against the establishment. Shortly after that, Tom originated the Lone Wolf action—a brilliant and frighteningly efficient strategy within which people with racist beliefs and ideals would secretly invade all parts of America, just waiting for the right moment to destroy the United States government and start over on their own terms. In his last trial, he said it all. "The White Separatist Movement will not be stopped in the puny town of Portland," Tom said passionately. "We're too deep, we're imbedded now. Don't you understand? We're in your colleges, we're in your army, we're in your police forces . . . where do you think all these Skinheads went? . . . They've got the program; we planted the seeds."

Tom was correct; seeds had been planted. Men that I had studied and trained with for years were now lawyers, journeymen electricians, and professors with doctorate degrees at prestigious universities. In addition, I was not the only one who had learned to be better in combat from my United States military training. Aryan warriors were now in every one of the armed services and in many government offices. Dangerous, powerful, and successful seeds had been planted.

DOMESTIC DISTURBANCES

My mother became extremely impatient of Nicole sitting around in her house while she was at work all day. Nicole didn't bother trying to work, and she didn't contribute anything around the house either—she just hung out. That was tough, because I came from a family with a very hard-working ethic. I think the most difficult thing for my mom to deal with was Nicole's coldness, resentment, and downright hatred of her. Finally, she told me it was time for us to find a place of our own. I agreed. I was sick of Nicole and the whole situation with my family. I had to have a straight discussion with her. I made up my mind that it was time for us to split up. I felt a sense of responsibility for her, so I kept putting it off, but she didn't even try to do anything for herself or others. Except for the Movement, Nicole and I had absolutely nothing in common, and even then, she didn't have any of the goals or dreams that I had.

That night I came home to tell Nicole that as a couple we were through—it was simply over. Before I could tell her, however, she said she needed to talk to me, too. I let her speak first, thinking she probably had the same news for me and it would be easier this way. Instead, she told me she thought she was pregnant. Suddenly, sickeningly, I felt stuck. My strong desire to get out of our unhealthy relationship was circumvented by the responsibility I felt for the baby. Within a few days, we found a small apartment and moved out. I went to work for my dad so I could provide a good living for my family.

A few months passed, and I was heavy into planning the Aryan Fest. There were a bunch of Hammerskins and others in the area willing to help me get the concert going, including Jeremy Reinnman, Ashley Brown, Ed Le'Bate, and others. I started a fake group called Nationalist Skinhead Knights. The Knights had their own post office box and everything. I wanted the cops to think *they* were the ones putting on the concert. The idea was for this false organization to take all the heat so the Hammerskins could more easily organize the Aryan Fest without police intervention.

One day I got pulled over and I had a bunch of Aryan Fest concert flyers with me. I got out my driver's license and made it easy for the cop— I even showed him my tattoos. He told me he wouldn't write me a ticket if I told him about the flyers. I cooperated but told him as little as I could. "I'm trying to wake up white kids to problems in our society," I said. "We're just getting together to have some fun and a little education."

The cop eyed me. Suddenly I realized that someone had remembered who I was, and they were onto me again. "Look, it's been really quiet here since you've been gone," he said pointedly. "It's been really *nice*. We're not about to have a lot of shit going on here again, get it?" Soon I had cops tailing me wherever I went. I would go outside and they'd be there. It was almost as bad as before I left for the Marine Corps.

I made it a point to be friendly with the police. It bothered Nicole, who, like other Skins, called them ZOGs—Zionist Occupational Government soldiers—and she wondered why I was even talking to them. I told her that bullshitting with them wouldn't do any harm. Besides, I wanted to see what they knew. It never hurt to be a little friendly and usually worked to my advantage. I also knew from past experience that if I told them to piss off they could get really nasty. They could make our lives miserable, and it wasn't worth it. The big thing was to get the cops off our tail. I needed the freedom to recruit again, and the Aryan Fest was to be my biggest tool.

As time drew near to have our first baby, I was excited with the prospect of being a father, despite my rocky relationship with Nicole. When
our first son, Tommy, was born, we brought him home and hung a torrid
red flag of a white and black cross and large swastika above his crib. We
were excited to have given birth to a new generation of separatists, and
I continued heavily recruiting new Skins. The birth of my son started to
wake me up to the dangerous world I had created—but one eye was still
closed.

Tommy was born ten months before Aryan Fest. I celebrated by going
out with my friends to San Bernardino and getting wasted. I got my first
DUI since arriving back in the continental United States. Tommy was
just two days old. Around six months later, I was out driving and was
arrested by a San Bernardino County Sheriff. I was headed to a friend's
house, and we were going to take care of some business. I had my 9mm
with me, and during the search, the cop found it on me. I was booked in
San Bernardino County for carrying a loaded and concealed weapon.

The planning for Aryan Fest began in earnest. Unlike the Napa
area where Aryan Woodstock had been shut down, I learned that San
Bernardino could do open-air festivals. I secured a million dollar life
insurance policy. I made sure I got every single permit needed and followed the law to a tee—even down to the last portable potty. I used dona-
tions to create T-shirts. It took months and months, but we effectively
worked out every detail, knowing where and how we had our rights and
exactly how to operate so the cops couldn't touch us. The media was
going crazy because we weren't letting them know a thing, unlike last
time. Every controllable factor was put into place. We arranged to have a
band from Sweden, one from England, and four bands from the United
States to come and play. Our budget was the only sour note. As much as I
wanted the biggest band in the States and Europe to play, we didn't have
the money to attract them.

In addition, I was smart enough not to get Tom Metzger involved. I
knew that, like with Heick, he would try to take over and turn everything
into a circus so he could get the media attention he wanted. However, I
wanted the event to be successful and controlled, so I left him out of it.
I knew all the laws and the rules. I learned how to rent out places before
the owners got the whole story, such as getting a contract just a few days
before the event so the owners would not have enough time to shut us
down. Not only did I check out the life insurance policy, I checked out

every possible legal issue and what could be done in multiple open-air concert venues. If they could allow rock n' roll and country music to be out in the air, then they would have to allow others. I secured a place out in the middle of the desert. I put down "rock and roll gathering," with five hundred people attending on five acres of land, including enough portable toilets for five hundred people. I refused to get tripped up on even one item. If anything, I overplanned for every contingency.

My strict no-news policy kept the media in the dark except for the misinformation I was giving. It was tough to keep secret. I was gaining notoriety from all corners of the earth, it seemed, as people called from all over the world wanting to come to the concert.

My mother was delighted to have a grandchild, but Nicole had iced her desire to be the doting grandmother she always wanted to be. Rarely did Nicole let my mother see Tommy for more than a few minutes. The night of the concert, however, we knew we were going to be partying, so Nicole let my mother take baby Tommy. Mom figured something big must be going on, since historically she was Nicole's last resort, and she was right, since all the other Skins were at the concert. When my mother learned about the concert, it freaked her out, especially the realization that such big names in the White Power Movement were coming from all over the world and calling me, wanting to attend. I think it was the first time she realized that my influence was powerful enough to extend far beyond California. Even though it frightened her, I honestly thought it was way cool.

All in all, the Aryan Fest in Phelan, California, was a great show, out in the desert on five acres of land. Held over the three-day Labor Day weekend in 1992, it went till the wee hours of the morning every day. No Remorse from England, Durwinger from Sweden, CIS (Christian Identity Skins) from Utah, Extreme Hatred, and several other local groups attended. There was a huge mass of people drinking, but the whole event was very non-violent, at least for Skins. There was only one fight, when a dozen Skinhead girls beat up a guy for bumping into a pregnant girl. They began to beat the crap out of him before we broke it up and settled the issue ourselves. He was "kindly" asked to leave and given no choice in the matter.

Well over three hundred people came and partied at the Aryan Fest. One reporter found out about it and showed up, camera and all.

"You had better leave while you still can," I said pointedly. My look and my tone of voice said, "You'd better go now or you will not make it out alive."

"But I was invited by the guy putting it on," he protested.

"Bullshit!" I said, and shoved him. "I'm the guy putting it on, and you were *not* invited." The reporter, alive and well and ticked off, began his own misinformation strategy. He reported that no one had come to this event and said it wasn't worth mentioning. We knew better. The good news was that by the time anyone else from the media found out about it, it was too late to shut it down, too late to censor anything, and too late to kick us out until the party was over.

The only thing that sucked about the event is that we didn't make any real money. Everything was bought and paid for, and we made some profit off the shirts but not enough to pay for everything. We couldn't afford to pay the airfare for the bands that came from Europe. However, we were able to get them demo tapes of at least two songs to take back to Europe, and that helped reimburse their costs. Unfortunately, Rebellious Europeans released their American soundtrack as soon as they got back and were quickly rated and shut down by the French government. The racist message they were spreading was against French law. I loved being an American. I could be as hate-filled as I wanted to be, within reason, and I got away with it again and again.

Aryan Fest *was* successful in getting the racist movement "out there" in the public eye. It was the first successful concert of its kind outside of Oklahoma. From there, shows started popping up all over the United States. They learned from our successes and our mistakes. Promoters learned to purchase equipment instead of renting, or to rent certain items where it made more sense than building (like to rent a stage instead of building a stage that had to be thrown away). They learned from us that they could create a successful concert almost anyplace they wanted, as long as they got the proper permits and they stayed within the boundaries of the law. I often wonder if people would have ever continued to put on concerts in this arena if we hadn't been so successful. It certainly got a lot of publicity and brought in a lot of new recruits, right in line with my goals at the time. After that, eight or nine regional concerts were put on every year.

In the meantime, I turned to other profitable pursuits—namely recruiting people into Hammerskin Nation. The concert brought a certain renown to my name, and I was able to bring in masses of kids over the next several months. Their lives would never be the same.

10

Hook, Line, and Sucker: Effective Recruiting Tactics

DRUGS WERE ENTERING the gang scene more and more, even with Skinheads. Skins had been notoriously anti-drugs since their inception, but trafficking caught on with lightning speed because there was an insane amount of profit to be made. Older and committed Skins like me didn't want anything to do with them. We had seen drugs mess up people's lives and how it caused their thinking to be totally screwed up. They tended to make stupid decisions, become paranoid, and hurt their friends and families. What seemed even worse was the fact that they became incapable of following the code anymore. Everything we stood for didn't mean a thing to them. That disturbed me the most, I think.

There came a time of a huge rift between regular racists and green racists, or potheads—although pot usually wasn't the only drugs they dealt with. Cocaine, speed, LSD, mushrooms, ecstasy, heroine, and eventually meth were all part of the new world order. One chapter of green racists from San Diego who called themselves members of WHS were a particular thorn in my side. I felt they were a horrifying example of what it meant to be a Skin.

Therefore, after Aryan Fest I had a somewhat *new* obsession in which to put all my energy. I began recruiting *clean* kids into Western Hammerskins and then into Hammerskin Nation. WHS was the regional chapter, and almost anyone could join. However, only select people could become part of the elite Hammerskin Nation. For me, it was a way to play a game with them—to make sure they were committed and loyal. To make sure they stayed clean.

Recruiting became an everyday part of my life. I was obsessed. My mission was two-fold. First I wanted kids to see what I perceived was happening to their race and their culture. The other boiled down to creating more power for myself. Like before, the more kids I brought in, the more power I had. Particularly after Aryan Fest, I had a certain amount of power, control, and prestige. I wanted to keep it going. I had grown accustomed to this high authority and now I was ready to solidify it.

MAKING MYSELF THE MAN

A very effective tactic I used for recruiting was planting seeds of discord in schools in order to force in new recruits to whatever area we wanted. We'd sneak into a middle school or high school and post a bunch of flyers with harsh racial slurs against a particular ethnic group. As often as possible, we would find a way to put them in the lockers of ethnic kids and gangbangers. That racial group would react violently, jumping as many little white kids as they could in all their rage. Of course, the white kids would get tired of getting beat up, and they'd look somewhere for protection. My favorite part was just happening to be nearby, ready and welcoming. My friends and I were a safe harbor and a form of real protection for them. Suddenly I became the good guy. By offering our protection, I had just become their savior.

I also started attending town council meetings to draw attention to our cause. There were a lot of community and immigration issues going on. When Detective Dale Jensen first saw me there, I saw the blood drain from his face. He knew I was there to actively recruit people to my way of life—my violent way of life. Therefore, Dale also continued to attend these meetings to make sure I didn't create any additional heartburn in San Bernardino. He knew that Skinheads did not even claim to have the control over their minions as other white supremacist groups did. The fact that we loved hatred, aggression, and chaos for the sheer pleasure of it was most disturbing. He didn't know that I had "grown up" the theme and I wanted much, much more than a little chaos in one small sector of the country. I had bought into the rhetoric of bringing the entire nation to its knees. Still, he could tell there was something more to my schemes than a bit of harmful fun. Dale reported that I was a hazardous influence over an entire community because so many kids looked up to me, believed in me, and followed me blindly.

"Not very often do I see someone as influential as TJ," said Dale. "He was a propaganda preacher—much like the people the Third Reich sent out to entice the nation of Germany. And just as it was back then, rhetoric without knowledge makes a belief dangerous. TJ could suck them in so convincingly. He was one of the most dangerous people I'd ever met."

With my PR skills, I could bring intellectuals in as easily as I could thugs. I would explain to a group of smart folks that the Movement and my compatriots were a *reactionary* force.

"We are simply cleaning up the mess that others have created," I would say.

"Yeah, but aren't you white supremacists?"

"Nah, we're white *separatists*. We don't consider ourselves better than anyone else. You see all the violence taking place all around us; Bloods, Crips, Mexican Mafia . . . We just want to put a little distance between us, just go away from each other. They can have their shoot 'em up parties as much as they want—just so long as they leave us alone." Heads would begin nodding. People were tired of the violence and the inability of anyone to do anything constructive about it. Once I knew I had them sucked in, I pulled them with a few more half-truths.

"The police put us behind bars just for trying to clean up scum mess, like drug pushers, pimps, and dopers. The flag that flies in the courtyard of every jail and on every cop uniform is the flag of oppression. They're the ones imprisoning our brothers and sisters." As I kept going, it seemed to make more sense to them.

"Oh, we get it," would be the response, and I could tell they were genuinely ready to hear what I had to say next. Soon these same recruits would be watching for evidence of the government's involvement in sending Skins to jail, in letting minorities and Jews get off for crimes, and for any type of government corruption. Like us, whatever they were looking for they would find evidence of it. I would present it to them as often as possible too, in my own way. Giving them as much truth as I could, I would add a little spin. For example, my recorded hotline gave periodic updates of what was going on in the area. My messages were always meant to incite anger and discontent.

"Last week you might have heard that a college student was brutally raped up on campus," I would say. "What they didn't tell you is that she was raped by a black man . . ." Of course I would leave out certain information if it didn't help my case. I might not say that the woman was black or Hispanic or Asian. I would let them think what they wanted.

Teachers and other concerned individuals would often try to talk people out of listening to me. That was often a huge mistake. I could spout more statistics and historical facts than any teacher, pastor, or council member I had ever came across. Any argument they would try to bring up, from immigration to war crimes to historical facts, was easily debated and put down. A girl at Yucaipa High School was thinking about joining our group. Their teacher had made them read *Anne Frank: The Diary of A Young Girl*, and this girl wanted to do her book report on *Mein Kampf.* Her teacher went on a rampage. He ran into me with a group of Skins outside of the school.

"I want you to leave her alone," he snarled at me. "She's young and naive and gullible, and you're teaching her lies and a bunch of trash." I sized him up, and then gazed at him intently.

"I tell you what," I said amiably. "If you can tell me where Anne Frank died, I will leave her alone." He hesitated, taken aback. He couldn't tell me, but he didn't believe I would know it either.

"She died in Bergen-Belsen," I said smugly. "She was fifteen years old." I didn't add that she died of typhus and starvation in this work/transition camp where people were used up and then sent on to die at the concentration camps. I ended up making him look like a fool in front of a whole crowd. The girl got a Skinhead girl haircut the next day, and a few other people even joined her.

I taught my recruits how to write in runes so if they got caught, their teachers and parents would never know what they were writing. They loved how smart I was, and how stupid their parents, teachers, or other authority figures looked around me.

My boot camp training and my time in Hawaii had taught me how to more effectively break people down and build them up. I could take what I wanted from new recruits. I knew how to manipulate and control them. I knew how to exploit their weaknesses. I knew exactly what to do with their strengths. I could make them worship me because I *knew* what they were going through; I had already been there. I'd lived the life, I'd done all the things these kids were going to do, and I knew every story. Even the stupid ones.

Some of my new recruits had started wearing white power colors and insignias. I could tell they were going to get jumped. "Nah," they would say. Just like me at that age, they thought they were invincible. They thought nothing like that would ever happen to them. I just smiled, but I *knew* what was coming. Sure enough, a few days later several of my recruits were caught, cornered, and beat up. Nursing broken noses and other wounds, they were embarrassed and afraid I would ridicule them and come down hard. Sensing this, I took a different turn, knowing empathy would go a long way in earning their affections. I decided to tell them a story.

"Guys, we all make mistakes," I said, nodding at their surprised looks. "You're not alone."

"Yeah, right," one of them said. "I bet you never got beat this bad. We should've known better."

"Ah, hell, you guys haven't heard stupid till you hear this one," I laughed, nursing their wounded egos. "Long before I got married, I went to this club called *Your Place* in San Bernardino with Upland Dave and our girlfriends. My girlfriend wanted me to dance to every song, so we were out there shaking it up between every beer. I was already toasted, but I kept laying 'em back. It was getting crowded, and there were these two big black guys who were hip-hopping on the dance floor. We couldn't get past them. I got pissed off and bumped one guy—hard. He turned around and started to choke me. Dave slugged the guy. I yelled, 'You're a dead nigger, I say!'—which was about the stupidest thing I could have said, because the club was filled with 90 percent blacks!"

"Holy shit, what did you do?" they cried.

"Well, we sent the girls out to the car just as we started getting punched and pummeled. I ran this guy's face down a brick wall, pulling off his skin. Don't tell Dave I told you, but he was getting hammered by the other guy. This guy slammed the back of Dave's head into a water faucet, splitting his head wide open. Dave ran outside into the alley, even as people were still kicking and hitting him. The bouncers and I were trying to pull people off of him. Man, it was awful. Finally Dave and I made it to the car and jumped in. The girls took us to the hospital. That was an interesting ride, I'm telling you! I ended up with cracked ribs, and Dave was obviously in worse shape than I was. I can't tell you how many stitches he got—all because I couldn't keep my hands to myself or my mouth shut. But I learned my lesson. Now I don't do stupid shit like that anymore, and you won't either. You watch your backs all the time and only speak when you know you can make good on your threats. Make sure you're never outnumbered, create major destruction when you whip it up, and then get the hell out of there, got me?"

"Yeah!" they all roared. They loved me, except when they hated me.

I made sure that situations like this—and every situation, actually—made me appear in their eyes like the man with the knowledge and the power. They started coming to me and asking me questions. That's when I would throw out my new hook, line, and sinker: "Dude," I'd say, very seriously, "there's going to be a race war!" After I had told them the truth so many times, it was easy to give them a half-truth and some propaganda mixed in. They believed it. In fact, they ate it up. And they wanted to be on my side.

As well as I knew how to work the group, I also knew how to work each individual. If a kid liked to fight, *I* really liked to fight. All my experience as a chameleon gave me the skills to do whatever it was this kid needed to join the Movement. If a kid didn't like to fight, then of course, *I* didn't really like to fight, either. Then I would put them with others that didn't like to fight but were fabulous in the propaganda group, or in computers and technology. I would have them watch documentaries on white power or read books and teach other kids and suck them in that way. No matter what, I would find where their niche was.

Susan Spencer, a journalist for *48 Hours*, once called me a star recruiter for the Skinheads.

"What would distinguish the ones that you could turn from the ones that you couldn't?" she asked. My answer was simple.

"The ones I didn't talk to were the ones I couldn't turn," I said. It was true.

Rarely did it happen overnight, but I was patient. When I had them, I had them. I could take any average white kid and I could turn him into a Nazi in eighteen months to two years.

WORKING THE DYNAMICS OF THE CROWD

One of my favorite, solid recruitment tactics was a game I called Group A and Group B. Group A kids were rambunctious. They could kick ass and were not afraid to fight. Group B just wanted to belong. They liked the drinking, the partying, and the hanging out but weren't too keen on fighting. Unbeknownst to any of them, I had them pegged, and I would use group A against group B (and vice versa) to solidify their involvement.

When I had some really noncommittal member of group B, I would wait until the opportune time when both groups of kids were attending, especially after some kind of altercation. A perfect example of this was a party we had one night after a gang fight. I picked on Billy, the weakest kid from group B, who had not stepped up.

"What the hell is your problem, Billy?" I asked, my face two inches from his and absolutely menacing. "You didn't show up for your Aryan brother tonight when he needed you most!" He swallowed, but didn't say anything, his face ashen. "Show us you've got some balls!" I roared. "One of your brothers is going to get killed, and it will be *your* fault."

Billy stood there in shock, not knowing what to do. It was just as I expected. Without warning, I cold-cocked him in front of everyone. He hit the floor. Suddenly this Group B member had become the scapegoat for the night. I encouraged all the guys to spit on him, kick him, whatever struck their fancy. Some guy urinated on him, but that wasn't the worst of it. Billy got a couple of teeth knocked out and his nose was bleeding like crazy. We didn't stop until we got bored, and he was in bad shape. The rest of us sat down and had a couple more beers, laughing. When Billy came to, he used the furniture to drag himself up to a standing position and tried to leave quietly.

"You're a punk!" I yelled at him. "*Never* come around again."

Most of the time, these scapegoats would never come back. They'd be ridiculed and were forever blackballed. If a kid didn't come back, I'd grab another kid from group A like I did that night.

"Hey, TJ, *I'm* not a punk!" he cried. There was *no way* he wanted to be a B kid: beat up, ridiculed, outcast. So I invited him out with me and we pulled a drive-by shooting. It wouldn't matter—any kind of raging, random attack would fit the bill. At this point the new kid was dying to prove how hard-core he was, and he followed through perfectly (as they always did), with no hesitation. Even though he was shaking, I pretended not to notice. I took him back to the party to show off his valor and to reward him in front of every member there. They all got the lesson.

"I'm going to give you something great," I said. "I'm going to have one of the girls give you something very special . . ." I picked out the prettiest girl in the room and nodded for her to go back in the bedroom with him.

"Dude, I love you, man!" I said, watching him walk down the hall, his girl in tow. "You're awesome." He looked back at me and grinned. I had him for life.

Every great once in a while, one of the B kids *would* come back, only this time he'd be incredibly vicious and mean, which was just what I wanted in the first place. He would do exactly as I wanted him to, whenever I wanted it. He would make sure he was never a B kid again. In one night, I had just mentally twisted his psyche and made everyone in the room a more committed, obedient Skin.

MUSIC TO STOP THE WORLD
FROM TURNING

I continued to use the most effective technique to bring kids in, which was music. I was not the first recruiter to use music to indoctrinate kids about racism and white power, nor was I the last. Huge music labels continue to make tons of money using white power and hate-filled, Aryan messages, getting kids as young as grade-schoolers to listen to racist rhetoric.

I recognized the power of music at a very young age. I saw it as the most powerful influence in the world, especially on teenagers. I witnessed the effect of music every day. A friend's kid started listening to country music, and in two weeks he was strutting around in cowboy boots, flashing a belt buckle the size of Texas. I saw punk music affect kids all the time. Even a really conservative kid would end up with black hair or some other crazy hairdo. In another month he would become hardly recognizable as far as his energy and spirit.

Any time I possibly could, I would get a kid listening to white power music—especially the fast-paced, heart-pounding music that they liked, and soon enough he would be embodying, believing, and spouting all kinds of racist verbiage. Then I could get him to pass out a hundred tapes or CDs to all his friends. If anyone protested at first, we would say, "Hey, this is just white music by white kids for white kids!" It was part of all that good propaganda I learned to set up. Dave called it something else.

"You're a spin monster!" he said proudly. He loved to listen to me talk to kids and crowds. I could twist and turn *anything* to our advantage, and I did it at every opportunity.

11

BLOOD IS THICKER THAN WATER

WITH ARYAN FEST being over and a new baby in my home, my family asked me what I was going to do for money—legitimately, at least, now that I had become a father. I began working a bit in the telecommunications field for my dad. He had stopped working as a trucker and started his own telecommunications company, which was quite successful. I began making decent money, at least. I was also hiring Skinheads to come work for me. It looked to them like I had a lot of money, which wasn't true now that I had a family to support, but it continued to give me the appearance of control and power.

The different factions of Hammerskins (Eastern Hammerskins, Western Hammerskins, Confederate Hammerskins, and so forth) had continued fighting amongst themselves, and a new, deadly rivalry had reared its ugly head. The national Hammerskin leader, Sean Tarrant, finally came up with a strategy to diffuse the tension between the factions.

"We are all brothers under Hammerskin Nation," he declared. That was that. The man had spoken and no one could, or would, go against it. Guys now had a club logo tattooed on one arm and a Hammerskin Nation logo on the other. This large group encompassed literally thousands of people across the nation. Within this framework, I had a bigger vision—I wanted to see all Skins claim more solidarity, more power, and a bigger voice. In my own mind, I could see that a unified front (without territories) was the smartest thing to bring to pass. I thought about how our goals could really be accomplished if we all struck together. I thought about how the world would *have* to stand up and take notice.

I figure I had brought in at least eighty kids to the Movement by the time I became the regional recruiter for Hammerskin Nation. I only had to listen to two people above me (and half the time they listened to me). In Southern California, I probably had five to six hundred Skins who knew I was their superior. I was one of the elite Skinheads. My friends were rarely challenged, and when someone did challenge them, I threatened him and he backed off immediately. I had the reputation that I would rather eliminate problems than deal with them. If I needed to, I could have someone else eliminate my problem for me. I knew people in every place in the United States: Mississippi, Texas, Oklahoma, Minnesota; everywhere the Movement had a presence, or even the shadow of one, I knew the people involved. It was an unspoken agreement that we did things for each other.

From the late eighties to the early nineties, Hammerskins had been involved in serious crimes across the country. The Confederate Hammerskins in Texas and Oklahoma chased and beat blacks and Hispanics to intimidate them into staying out of Hammerskins territory. They had vandalized synagogues and a Jewish community center; firebombed a minority-owned nightclub and assaulted its non-white patrons; firebombed a residence mistaken for the home of rival Skinheads; assaulted two black girls; and even murdered two innocent black men—one in Texas and one in Alabama. These were just the crimes that Confederate Hammerskins became notorious for and were caught at. It doesn't include what wasn't known, or the violence in the North, West, and East.

WHS was picking up the pace in California. Due to increased publicity once again, not only through *WAR* networks and affiliates but through the regular media as well, we were rapidly increasing in numbers again—enemies, each other, and the police. When we were out, we were in constant danger, no matter who was in the car with us. For that reason, I began going out less and less. I didn't want something to happen to Nicole or Tommy.

As my son began to grow, I wanted to spend more and more time with him. I began to mellow out. If it weren't for the birth of Tommy, I would have been in a prison somewhere, rotting away. I was still getting arrested, but not anything like before—just for fighting or concealed weapons. For the first time in years, I wasn't going out looking for danger.

WHEN FRIENDS EQUAL TROUBLE

As much as I didn't go looking for trouble anymore, it still came looking for me. From time to time, a friend would call me up in a deep mess, and I was under a brotherhood obligation to assist him.

One night, Jeremy called to inform me that the IWB (Insane White Boys, whose territory was in Stanton and stretched out near Cyprus), was messing with him over some issue. It really didn't matter what it was—they had stepped over the line. Again.

When I hung up the phone, my friend Marty Cox was already on his way. Marty and I were like brothers, and we watched each other's backs. We knew what was coming. We went over to Skinhead Phil's house and drove in two separate cars. Marty and I were in my truck, and Phil ended up going with Paul in his car. I had my twelve-gauge shotgun, and we were heading out to terminate as many IWB as we could. Unless the cops were on my tail, I generally didn't go anywhere without my AR-15 rifles, both SKS rifles, and both 9mm handguns. It wasn't unusual to have three hundred rounds of ammunition within arm's reach (or at least in the trunk). This night, however, we were being careful of "the rules" and had the others in our group in the other car. The others were felons, and we had rules about felons down to a tee. We knew exactly what to do and what not to do to keep everybody out of jail and prison.

First, we went to a pool hall where the IWB were known to hang out in Stanton. No one was there, and we were sorely disappointed. Plan B became a drive-by at Dave Dosset's house, also in Stanton, and we headed over there. As we neared the home, we saw someone else walking in. We whipped our car around quickly, preparing to open fire. We heard Paul shout, "Don't do it!" Marty pulled my gun out anyway. Just as he was about to cut loose, two Orange County Sheriff's cars turned the corner. We picked up speed but knew we'd been tagged. Paul stopped his car and quickly got out. He walked through the gate like he lived there, as a decoy for us. He knew we needed time to stash our weapons. It was too late. The cops lit me up. I was blinded by their search lights and held my hands over my eyes and well within their sight. I didn't need to be blown away by a cop tonight.

Luckily, Marty had hidden the weapon under his seat really well. The cop asked me for my license and registration. I was in BIG trouble. I didn't have a license at the time; I'd lost it with the last DUI. Marty had the same problem. To make matters much worse, he got out of the car. We had both been told not to move. The OC Sheriffs pointed the gun at him and growled, "Make a wrong move, and you're dead!" They pulled Marty roughly over to the patrol car to question him, separating us. Then they tried to get me to reveal where the gun was.

"What gun?" I asked, playing innocent. "Look, man, there's no gun."

In the other car, they were asking Marty the same questions. He told them we were just coming to see our friend Dave. (The ironic thing is that we really *used* to be friends with Dave until he joined IWB.) The cops thoroughly searched our car and didn't find a gun in there. One of the cops, however, would not accept it. He threw a huge fit. It would have been almost comical if I wasn't trembling. If they found the gun, I was up a creek, and I knew it. I forced myself to stay calm, even as the police officer was screaming.

"Look, I've run both these guys," he shrieked. "There are guns. I KNOW there's a freaking gun in that car!" These officers were getting smart in finding our guns and alcohol. We had learned to hide handguns and ammo anywhere and everywhere. It wasn't unusual for a Skin's car to be fully loaded at times: guns in the airbag boxes, behind the plates, tied to the hood, in the fake boxes in the doors, in the backseat up in the springs, and so forth. They had to look hard, but they were getting smart. (One thing they never found was our jungle juice or other alcohol we stashed in the windshield wiper fluid dispenser. We had it rigged so when we drove around town, all we had to do was push the wiper fluid dispenser and it would squirt right into our mouths. We could get drunk as we drove and cops never could find the source of alcohol or get the young ones for possession.)

With renewed determination, the sergeant bent down and slowly, methodically felt up into the springs under the seat. I saw his arms go down and then up. *Oh, no,* I thought. *It's over.* Sure enough, he pulled my gun out and held it up.

"Hey, what's this?" he asked as he cocked the gun. The round was chambered. He looked at me, his face smug. "Whose gun is this?"

"It's my gun," I said firmly. What I didn't know was that in the other police car, Marty said it was *his* gun, so we were both arrested and herded into a squad car to be booked for a loaded, concealed weapon.

As we took off, the back door wasn't fully shut and started to come open as we rounded the corner.

"Hey," Marty joked, "if the door opens all the way and we fall out, are we free to go?" There was no response. Just an ominous click.

Marty was attempting to make light of everything since he was having trouble reading my face. He knew something was wrong. I was trying not to panic. This was my second loaded and concealed weapons charge—a felony. I was going to prison for at least a year.

During booking, I was amazed and dumbfounded (then of course, thrilled) to find out how faulty the law enforcement communications system in California really was. The department in Orange County knew absolutely nothing about my previous weapons charge, due to the fact that it had occurred in San Bernardino County. It took everything I had not to jump up and down in sheer happiness. No prison.

In the Orange County Sheriff's Department, there was a hallway with a bench and speaker phones so the officers could hear everything that was said. Marty and I both got to make a call. Marty went first.

"Hey, babe," he began talking to his wife, "I've been arrested. I'm at the Orange County Sheriff's Department—"

Kari started freaking out.

"What the hell?" she started screaming at him, her voice shrill with rage through the receiver. "I *told* you not to go with those guys! I *told* you not to go shooting out—" Marty hung up on her. This time it was the cops who were enjoying the joke.

I called Nicole, praying under my breath that she would not give me the same response.

"Do I need to come bail you out?" she asked when I had explained where I was.

"No," I breathed in relief. "I'll just stay here." From previous experience, we both knew it was a lot cheaper for us to do it this way. At least she knew why I wasn't coming home and that I was safe. I asked the officers if I could make another call, and got Chris, a Skinhead girl, to pick me up the next morning and take me to the impound place to pick up my car. Marty was forced to stay because he had a previous warrant for his arrest in the county.

All my associates had more time than money. If any of us got a speeding ticket or a DUI, we always claimed poverty and asked to spend time in jail. We always requested a weekend too, if possible, claiming some kind of job during the week. The fact was, the jail was all booked up on the weekend. We'd go up to Glen Helen, where they would have us sign in, take our picture, and send us home. They didn't have time to process us for six hours and six more to process us back out. All we had to do was to learn the system and utilize it to our advantage.

NEVER GET OUT

After my arrest, I remember one kid who was worried about me, saying, "You can't be a Hammerskin anymore."

Yeah, right! Who the hell are you to tell me that? I thought. The cops were bad enough to have as enemies, but turning away from the Skins? No way. Although Skins tended to be a looser network than some Hispanic gangs or others with the "Blood In, Blood Out" mentality (meaning you're in for life—if you leave, you die), as an elite Skinhead with connections across the country, my situation was fairly similar. My mind raced to one of those powerful connections in Texas. *Sure. Let's call up Liz Tarrant and you tell her I'm out.* Liz was Sean Tarrant's wife. Sean was the powerfully successful Skinhead leader who went to jail after instigating nine years of racial beatings, attacks, and burnings in Texas. (Sean and his buddy Daniel "RIP" Rouch vouched for me and promoted me to a Hammerskin member and leader.) Cops learned of a gruesome conspiracy to annihilate the Jews in a local synagogue, using cyanide in the air ducts and chains on the doors so no one could escape. With Sean's incarceration, his wife, Liz, became a white power figurehead. She got everything straight from Sean, and she led the Movement from the outside—as effectively as her husband had when he was out. These guys didn't take any crap from anyone. They were rough people, and only two of all the people who wouldn't take kindly to me leaving.

I couldn't help but think of the sheer, brute force of many Skins. A former friend of mine, Frank Tocash, was a Hammerskin who had beat up a guy one night just because this guy "happened to get in the way." The victim's brain swelled so bad that doctors had to shave off part of his brain tissue in order to save his life. Since Skins don't take kindly to people who just get in their way, I couldn't imagine how they would feel against anyone in power who broke the oath and left the Movement. I remember thinking, *Don't bother trying to get out—or you'll get seriously messed up. They don't forget. They never forget.*

My brother Phil entered the San Bernardino's County Sheriff's law enforcement academy shortly after being discharged from the Marine Corps. I thought it was hilarious that we had the traditional Irish-Catholic family of cops and convicts. It wasn't as easy for Phil, however. He had to take an intensive course over several months for his training. As part of the academy, they covered issues with California gangs as extensively as possible. First they covered black gangs like the Bloods, Crips, and Pirus. Then Hispanic gangs such as the Mexican Mafia and Nuestra Familia, and then rapidly growing Asian gangs. Finally, they covered white gangs including white supremacists and separatists, biker gangs, the Armenian and Russian mafias, and white prison gangs. They covered whites from East Valley, Redlands, and Yucaipa areas.

Phil was taking meticulous notes as the instructor was talking.

"Just as we've told you with every ethnic group so far," said the instructor, "with the white gangs, there are a few local pains in the ass we'd really like to put in prison." Phil felt his lunch come up in his stomach.

"The biggest pain in the ass of any white supremacy group, including Skinheads and Hell's Angels, is TJ Leyden. This silver-tongued bastard is a recruiter and mastermind of Western Hammerskins, and we think he's recruiting for Hammerskin Nations as well . . ."

Most people continued furiously scribbling notes, but a few looked up at Phil, checking out his nametag and putting two and two together. Not too many Leydens around. Although Phil did his best to hide his nametag for the rest of the day, a few people cornered him after class.

"Hey, buddy, you don't happen to be related to this TJ Leyden, do you?" they asked, joking and smiling.

"Yeah," he whispered, hoping no one else would hear. He already had to reveal everything he knew to the academy and Rialto PD, his prospective employers. "Yeah. TJ is my crappy brother."

12

DRUGS, DECEPTION, AND DISILLUSIONMENT

LIFE PROCEEDED ON the way it was for a while, but I was too well known in California by Skins, anti-Skins, and law enforcement. In 1992, I began seriously thinking of going to Utah to recruit for Hammerskin Nation. Several reasons prompted this. If Nicole and I moved there, I could recruit without the police on my tail every second—at least for a while. I didn't have a record in Utah, and there weren't as many people to go to war with or as many friends in trouble to drag me into it. Another good reason is that we were supposed to hook up with some big-name people with some big money. That never hurts a cause.

Nicole was anxious to move to a "whiter" state, and we definitely had sympathizers in Utah. Though our Aryan wedding was not legal in California, it didn't matter with cohabitation laws. Utah was another set of circumstances altogether, with much more rigid laws. So, after moving to Washington County, Utah, we became legally married. As a young father, I was looking to be a better dad too. I figured I could do a better job away from the temptation of violence and the everyday madness of my home state.

California really *was* getting crazy, and the Skins were behind more chaos than the cops or the community ever suspected. In fact, a race war was nearly started in California during the time of the LA Riots. People don't know how close we came to inciting an all-out race war. If Tom Metzger hadn't put the brakes on the Skinheads, the world would be very different today. For a family who knew what was coming down, it was time to get out.

BIG NAME, BIG ADDICTION

We began getting to know the big-name people in the Movement out-side of California that we wanted to be involved with—or at least who we initially thought we did. We were told that Johnny Bangerter was a great mover and shaker in the White Power Movement in Utah—a Midwest coordinator of sorts. His family claimed a lot of financial and political power in the state. Johnny and his immediate family also claimed affilia-tion with Aryan Nations. Their friends boasted that one of the Bangerter children had even been baptized by Pastor Richard Butler of the Church of Jesus Christ Christian, better known as Aryan Nations.

The Skins in California talked about how Johnny and his buddies were such good friends to the cause and were surely up-and-coming lead-ers for a national front. Even my friend Bobby "Trigger" Seamens (who had once been my deadly enemy during the Skinhead Wars, long before Hammerskin Nation) assured me that Johnny Bangerter was an "okay" guy. Trigger was living in St. George and was married to Johnny's sister, and everything seemed to fit. I decided it was time.

I moved out and left Nicole and Tommy in California. I got a job in my forte, telecommunications, and put down a deposit on an apartment right away. Then I sent for my family. Wearing long-sleeved and collared business shirts by day, I played the consummate businessman. At night in my wife beaters and T-shirts, I got to know Johnny and his stepfather very well. Within a few more weeks, I wished I didn't know either one of them at all.

The first time I caught Johnny doing drugs, he admitted it.

"Look, I'm just smoking a little marijuana," he protested. "It's only a little pot now and then." It's amazing how fast I felt trapped. What was I going to do? I'd already been in St. George for two months, and my family had just arrived. Trigger admitted to me that he didn't like it either. He revealed another layer of deceit by telling me that Johnny and his stepfather were using methamphetamines and cocaine in addition to pot. I'd taken off from California to get *away* from the dopers and meth heads, and now I was smack in the middle of them again.

Even worse, it took only a short time to determine that Johnny was essentially crazy already. On top of that, the drugs served to make him absolutely paranoid and dangerous. Not only was he a big-time cokehead, but he was also an enemy to true Skinhead principles. Johnny was a drug runner.

In the eighties and early nineties, Skins thought anyone dealing drugs were a class below them. I especially didn't like the drug scene or anything it stood for. I wasn't about to change my mind here, no matter what big name I was dealing with.

I did my best to ignore Johnny's drug abuse, but my heart wasn't in it. Nicole had gotten really close to Johnny's wife, and so she would go over to visit her often. After work, I would end up spending time at their home—far more time than I ever would have wanted. Nicole even had a "white power baby shower" at their house. Like all Aryan warriors, their family wanted an army of young kids to be raised from the time they were born to be vicious killers. Johnny's mother homeschooled all the children and taught them Aryan doctrine. To an outside Skin, this might all seem fine and well, but drugs, Skins, and leadership don't mix. This guy was supposed to lead fifty Skin soldiers in the Movement. I couldn't shake the feeling of impending doom.

In St. George, I felt stuck, disillusioned, and incredibly disappointed. I was furious with Trigger for lying to me about the situation. "I didn't want to tell you when you got here, TJ," he said. "Johnny, his stepdad, the Skins—they're all pieces of crap." Johnny bugged the hell out of me; a self-proclaimed neo-Nazi who was nothing but a dark and dirty drug runner, and a sham as a father. He was so paranoid and cheap that he moved four times in the eighteen months we were down there. He never paid full rent. He had a system down, and he would simply leave and not look back. I think what bugged me the most was what he was teaching his kids—and not teaching his kids—through his example.

By this time in the evolution of the Movement, I knew two dozen dirty Skinheads for every clean one. Johnny had to be one of the dirtiest I ever met. In addition to the drugs, his gun running was lending itself into a vigorous trade. For all the risk he was taking, Johnny and his family never got anything out of it because all the profits went to support his drug habit. Since he could get guns really cheap, Johnny suggested to me that I could help fence the guns for a lot of money. No way—I knew I could get in a hell of a lot of trouble for running guns. I had my own *legal* arsenal. I wasn't about to sell his stuff and become a criminal. (Okay, I already was one, but not in gun running.) More adamantly, I refused to get sucked into anything that would feed anyone's drug habits.

Although Johnny was a loudmouth, I don't think the cops were too wise about me. They knew Trigger and I were hanging around there, but it was fairly obvious that they didn't know the extent of our vast criminal behavior. If the St. George law enforcement had contacted California, however, it would have been a much greater challenge to live and operate. This was particularly true since I wasn't without my own problems during that length of time.

After my family and I had settled in St. George for a few months, I visited California for a week to take a telecommunications class. I happened to be driving down the freeway when I heard that several Skins got busted from a group I knew quite well—the Fourth Reich. Reports said members of Fourth Reich were caught planning to bomb a Jewish synagogue and an AME African church. They were busted for illegal guns and pipe bombs. On the radio, they started listing the names of those arrested. One person's name stuck out—my friend Jeremy Reinnman.

I switched lanes and quickly drove over to Jeremy's house to check it out. He was there, out on bail.

"Do you remember that day we were together and I sold that gun to that pastor?" he asked. I remembered an old guy, calling himself the Reverend something-or-other from the World Church of the Creator, who had come looking for us. We had a short conference with him, but not before we ran this guy's name. We couldn't find *anything* on him. In fact, he was so clean he didn't exist! (Tip-off one.) A group of us sat around a table with him while he asked us crazy questions, like asking if we could get guns off a military base. (Tip-off two.) He was an idiot, but we didn't let him know that we knew it. This was too dangerous a game. It was far better to let the Feds or rival gangs hang around—and know what they were asking for—than to let them know their cover had been blown. Jeremy was the only one tempted to continue negotiations. He obviously didn't take our advice to leave it alone.

"I remember telling you he was a Fed and you were going to get busted," I said. He couldn't look me in the eyes.

"Yeah, well," he said morosely, "he was definitely an undercover agent. That's why I got busted."

I don't believe Jeremy ever went to jail for it, however. Luckily for him, there wasn't a lot of evidence, although the Feds sure tried. In the indictment, my name was listed, along with Dave and Paul. We were people they were dying to nab. They knew there was more to us and our involvement, but there wasn't enough evidence. Some people like Jeremy wouldn't listen to common sense and had to learn the hard way. Johnny

Bangerter was another one who didn't always listen to common sense, and racists in Utah had to pay for his mistakes.

On more than one occasion, I heard Johnny publicly vow that he planned to lead his army of Israel Skinheads to take over Zion National Park.

"If anything ever happens," he cried, "we're going to Zion! It's a soldier's paradise. I could hide out here and hit my targets pretty easy."

"You're wacked!" I said. "You don't have *any* position of power in the Park. It would take very little time for them to run you out." Now, if he had been a sniper, that would have been another situation, but he wasn't a good shot.

"What do you think about training?" I asked him seriously. "Do you really want to train?" There were guys I knew that would come out to St. George immediately to teach him how to become a seasoned sniper, but he wouldn't do it. He was too busy getting high and paranoid.

One night, about three or four in the morning, Johnny called me on the phone, screaming at me to come over to his house right away.

"TJ, you gotta get over here!" he cried. "The FBI is casing my house, man! The Feds are crawling all over my lawn." I hung up and stealthily drove toward his house, watching for cars, checking out the entire neighborhood. From my vast previous experience, I knew what surveillance looked like, and no one was anywhere near Johnny's home. I cautiously knocked on the door, making sure he could see me so he didn't blow me away by mistake (entirely too prevalent a possibility). Johnny ushered me in and peered carefully out the window.

"See?" he whispered, obviously hallucinating, "They're *everywhere* out there!"

"Johnny," I said, pushing him away from the window and onto the couch, "if the FBI was coming for you, they would have rented the house across the street. They would have had a surveillance team set up, a parabolic microphone listening into your conversations, and they would be building a case against you. They're not going to crawl all over the grass and get wet. They'll nab you in the open, or simply come and serve you a warrant."

I couldn't believe how far this regional Movement leader had sunk into his delusions. He had become more paranoid since his friend, Randy Weaver, had his standoff in a mountain cabin in Idaho with a U.S. Federal Marshall. Randy had been a fellow racist who was wanted on gun running charges. His wife and thirteen-year-old son were caught in the standoff crossfire and killed. Shortly after, singing at a white power concert, Johnny had clearly declared war on the federal government. That was when he had also decided that Zion National Park was the battleground. It didn't help that he was constantly talking to the media about his wild ideas; I'd heard him on several occasions.

"We are for the Second Amendment which allows the American people to arm themselves," he said on camera. "And when we take over, we're going to level the IRS building." (Nothing like building a lot of confidence in the public for the Second Amendment.) He also dogmatically proclaimed, "I'll shoot a U.S. Marshall. I'll shoot an FBI agent. I'll shoot an IRS agent. They're the enemies, to me. They're the enemies of Yahweh. And as far as I'm concerned, I'll deliver them a high-speed subpoena, and they *will* show up in court." Johnny might not have had Feds crawling on his lawn, but public comments like that didn't exactly foster a lack of suspicion, either.

I left after only eighteen months. I took Tommy, Nicole, and our new son, Konrad, back to California. As hard as I had tried recruiting around Johnny, or recruiting other people not affiliated with him, it didn't work. Everyone with any Skin affiliation or promise was either family to Johnny or just as big a methhead as he was.

I wasn't surprised later to hear Johnny was arrested on weapons charges a few years later. Apparently the judge only slapped his hands and sent him on his way. Soon after, however, Johnny, his wife, brother, and another woman were arrested on drug charges at the Bangerters' home near St. George for alleged possession of methamphetamine and drug paraphernalia. Johnny's six kids were left home alone in what the Poverty Law Center called "a ramshackle affair with no electricity beyond an extension cord from a neighbor's house." That didn't surprise me either, although it made me sad. From what I knew of Johnny, every cent he had went to meth and stolen guns. Fortunately, his children were placed in their grandparents' custody. I hoped that was better for them than the nightmare I perceived they had been living through.

Some people wouldn't believe that as a Skinhead I had any standards. Perhaps it seemed like an oxymoron since I had very *few* standards, but anything involving drugs or harsh treatment of kids was where I drew the line.

13

ONE STEP FORWARD, TWO STEPS BACK

IN FEBRUARY OF 1994, our second son, Konrad, was born. Again we were looking at our options in other states, even as we were working to survive back in California. Our family had first come to live with my mom until we got back on our feet—on her condition that our cats stay outside. Unfortunately, Nicole kept letting them in, and they were literally tearing up my mother's furniture. Finally, Mom said we had a choice—get rid of the cats or get out. That's when we moved in with my dad. He let us have a room until the first of April, when we got into our own apartment in Yucaipa.

Many things seemed to be good: our little family was growing, we were hanging out with old friends, and I was working for my dad making good money. I liked being able to pay all my bills. Though Tommy and Konrad shared a room, they were still young, and financially we were in the best shape of our married lives. The only dark spot was that my relationship with Nicole was getting worse. Still, my love for my boys was growing steadily. I *loved* being a dad. It was the only time since Marine boot camp that I felt passion and focus. I wanted to raise my sons well. Every time I looked at them, I was so proud and excited to be a father.

Soon after our move, Nicole and I took Tommy and Konrad to a birthday party at Tonya's house in Fontana. Tonya was a Skinhead girl, and the party was for her daughter. About a dozen grown-ups and several kids showed up to join in the celebration.

Everyone was having a great time. The kids were involved in all of the games you would expect at a young child's party. I found myself intrigued, watching these cute kids figure out their world, watching the process of learning and discovering. As Tommy played Pin the Tail on the Donkey, I was proudly thinking what a smart little cuss he was. He was amazing to me, and Konrad would be literally following in his footsteps soon. Tommy was always asking questions about the world and how it worked, and in spite of my cynical views, I often found myself being fascinated with certain things that had never held my attention before. For the first time since my own childhood (and because of that trauma, perhaps the first time ever), I began seeing things through the eyes of a child. I found it a profound, life-changing experience to be a father. Although I had become a very cold man, hardened to 99 percent of the world, these two little guys were thawing a piece of me deep inside . . . making me discover parts of myself I hadn't realized even existed. I was feeling love.

My train of thought was broken as we were invited to go outside for the pinnacle of the party, the last big game before cutting the cake and going home. I was excited for Tommy, since he had never encountered a piñata before. Like every dad, I secretly wanted him to be the one to break it wide open, and to watch his face when the prizes and candy spilled out. This was going to be fun.

Skinhead Phil brought the piñata out and carried it through the crowd. The grown-ups started laughing hysterically, and I moved in for a closer look, expecting a brightly-colored clown with a funny face or something equally childish and amusing. Instead, the piñata was in the form of a little black man. While his costume was brightly colored, he had black hands and feet, and a clearly defined black face. He wasn't to be hung by a string or cord, either. Around his neck hung a large rope strung into a noose.

I laughed along with everyone else until Phil threw the rope up into the tree, and started to haul the piñata up by the neck, the noose still strung about it. My stomach turned. I did not like what I was feeling here. Instead of one child at a time taking turns, all of the children were being given sticks and had already started to beat at the piñata while the grown-ups laughed. They thought it was hilarious, but as a stick was being handed to Tommy, I had the urge to shout out. My laughing, jeering buddies would think I was nuts, but something about this felt *wrong*.

I walked over to grab the stick from Tommy, but surprisingly Nicole actually beat me to it.

"No!" she told Tommy firmly. "You will not do this." A few people who heard her were shocked.

"Yeah, guys, this is stupid!" I backed her up. "Incredibly stupid and ignorant. We know better than this."

Everything stopped and the children lowered their sticks for a moment. They heard something in my voice and knew I was serious.

"Aw, c'mon!" a couple of the grown-ups yelled. "What's the big deal? This is so funny! This is cool!"

"No, it's not!" I shook my head vehemently. "We don't want to teach this to our kids and have them go to school and take a baseball bat and bash some black kid's head in with it. They'll end up going to jail. We're *smarter* than that."

I was relieved to know that Nicole agreed with me on this point, at least somewhat. I overheard her talking to several girls in the group. "Stuff like this is going to get our kids in trouble," she said. "If it was just us as adults, it would be cool. But the kids don't know any better."

Looking around, I wondered how many kids in the group had also heard her say that. I was reminded of the double standards my dad always had for me and my brothers. He could do certain things that we were never allowed to, yet his example spoke louder than words. I began to shift uncomfortably as we got ready to leave and go home.

Somewhere in the twisted recesses of my mind, I did not like the influence of this game, these people, and their stupid ideas upon *my* child. Sure, I wanted my kids to be racists. I just wanted them to be smart, *intellectual* racists. I didn't want them to be thugs and thieves and idiots. I was seeing and judging everyone else's influence on my children. What I wasn't seeing was my own.

While I had slowed up a bit in being a conservative, working dad, I was still taking chances in everyday life as if it were no big deal. WHS went to Aryan Fest that year in the Angeles National Forest. I wasn't part of any of the planning in 1994 except what our group was going to do there, but that was involvement enough. No one was supposed to bring guns, but my buddies and I went packing heavy. We were sure there was going to be a big rumble between many of the Skin groups. Sneaking my 9mm in, I was prepared for a shootout at the very least, and absolute mayhem if it looked like it might break loose. Each Skin group always had a sergeant of arms, and sure enough, the different clan sergeants were there, and with my seasoned, military-trained eye, I knew they were *not* clean.

Miraculously, though many death threats were made that night between Hammers and the Front, everyone walked away without a scratch. Were things finally mellowing out a little between rival factions? I mulled it over in my mind. Evidence seemed to point to something a little less noble: Skins cared more about drugs than any ideals or competition.

WELFARE AND WARFARE

In the spring of 1994, when Tommy was a little over two, we all went together to collect welfare from the lovely and generous state of California. Like so many Skin couples, we were pros at partaking of whatever the state would give us. We'd done it for years before we were legally married. Nicole sat down at the desk with Tommy, and I left to take Konrad in order to change his diaper.

When I came back, Nicole gave me a nervous glance.

"Take Tommy outside," she whispered urgently. "Right away!"

"Why?" I asked her, confused at her alarm. I felt for my 9mm, and realized I had left it outside in the car. Carefully, Nicole motioned, ever so slightly to a family on the other side of the room.

"Tommy pointed to them," she said, her eyes flicking toward them and back at me. "He said, 'Look, Mommy, there's some niggers.' " The hair on the back of my neck stood straight up.

"Did they hear him say that?" I asked, fighting down the panic I saw reflected in her eyes. She shrugged, not knowing if they had heard him or not.

I glanced over at the family. They did not seem to be gang-related, at least in appearance—they certainly were not flashing any colors which was smart in this government office—and yet not one of them was looking at me in the eyes. I felt a nervous tension in the room, whether it was from them or just from us, I didn't know.

As quickly as I could, I picked Tommy up and took him outside with his baby brother. I needed to remove them from the situation, *and* to get them to my car, where my handgun was. I needed to protect them, to keep them safe. As I walked out of the building, I glanced in all directions. I was worried. I wasn't just some redneck punk from the sticks who had taught his kid to say that word out of ignorance. I knew what that word meant to black people. I knew what rage and frustration it could incite—I had used it purposefully all the time. Certain words could quickly cause almost *any* people to become violent. It didn't matter if the people were white, black, Hispanic, Asian, or what have you—particular words in every culture are warring words, battle cries. Before I had even shut my door, I pulled out my 9mm from its hiding place.

Nothing happened that day. Nicole finished handling her business, and when she came out alone, I breathed a sigh of relief. Still, I didn't put my gun back until the welfare office was several blocks behind us and I was sure that we were not being followed. Sure, nothing happened—except that I couldn't deny we had taught our child a word at two and a half that could have easily got him killed.

14

GULLAH GULLAH ISLAND AND OTHER "COLOR-FUL" TALES

BY AUGUST OF 1994, it was apparent that Nicole and I were only together for the sake of the boys. I kept thinking that I couldn't keep doing this just for the kids when we were both miserable. There was simply nothing left of our marriage to salvage, and the boys could sense our problems. The one thing I was truly grateful for at this point was the quality and quantity of time I was able to spend with my young sons. Tommy and Konrad were the joy of my life. I found myself wanting to provide for, nurture, and strengthen them in ways I hadn't been capable of before. I was pondering the deeper questions of life in a way I never had—pondering why I was here, what difference I had made in the world, and what kind of example I was being to my sons.

I brutally questioned my contribution. I *had* made a contribution, after all, and thousands of Skins knew it, and knew me as a great leader. But was it the kind of contribution I wanted my sons to grow up living? Most of the time I was sure. Sometimes, I wasn't.

I remembered the last pointed conversation I had with my mother.

"Tommy, if you really believe in that white power rhetoric, then you can't pretend not to believe that *I* should be murdered as well for my polio."

"Oh, Mom, not this again," I protested. It made me just as uncomfortable as the first time she had brought it up.

"Do you believe I'm 'less-than' because of something I can't control?" she asked pointedly. I really never had. My mom had proven to me how strong and capable she really was, and she had survived so many things in life already, including that disease. Once again, I couldn't answer her.

Would my kids grow up having "subhuman" judgments about their grandma? After all, they had been carefully indoctrinated from day one, and I had been so proud they were going to grow up as Aryan warriors like myself. Part of the issue was that I wasn't nearly as proud to be an Aryan warrior as I once was. In California, Hammerskin Nations was growing like crazy, but now it included a tragically large number of pot-heads mixed with warped Christian Identity people. They believed, "God created pot so it's okay to smoke it." That's why we called them "Green Racists." More than ever, everything in gang life had begun to revolve around the politics of drugs and drug running. Several of the old guys like my friend Marty hardly ever went out anymore. He'd go to my house or perhaps to another friend's to party, but wouldn't go anywhere else. He was right to feel a bit fearful.

One of my friends I had grown up with was Tom, who had become involved in PENI (Public Enemy Number 1), and from there had become involved in drugs. His buddies got paranoid and thought he had snitched on them. He was shot fourteen times. Dopers freak out on their drugs—it's a horrible fact in trying to deal with them. The paranoia was creating murder within our own ranks.

For me, it wasn't just the paranoia—it was the changing of the guard. The new leaders were using racism as a form of control over stupid, drug-induced minions. For the second time since I got back from the Marines I was having a hell of a time trying to recruit. My old "Come and hang out with us, party with us" wasn't working as well when I included, "By the way, there's no weed. And there's no meth." Damn it, they didn't want to come anymore. It seemed everyone wanted to do meth or pot.

Younger dope Skins were handling a lot of money through the drug trade and had assumed a lot of command they didn't have and hadn't earned. I felt they were getting too big for their britches. The power plays became so bad that they were telling me I couldn't run my hotline any-more, saying that I didn't have authorization.

"Why the hell do I need authorization?" I asked, belligerently. "I've been a Skin longer than you've been a racist! If you have a problem with it, make the call [to the national leaders]." They backed down, but I didn't know how long that would last. I was continually feeling more and more restless.

I didn't always like the direction the Movement was heading, but I was still proud of raising my children with the racist philosophy I believed in until one golden, illuminating morning in 1995. The questions and doubts I had were beginning to fester under my skin. They wouldn't let me feel any peace. That morning, Nicole was asleep in the bedroom. I got up with the boys to take care of them and feed them breakfast. I turned on a children's program to keep Konrad busy so he wouldn't wake his mother.

Before breakfast was ready, I was playing with Konrad when three-year-old Tommy walked into the TV room. *Gullah Gullah Island* was playing on Nickelodeon, and my toddler and I were listening to the Caribbean-flavored music and I was having fun watching him dance along with the characters. I hadn't paid much attention to anything else about it. Tommy, however, walked over to the television with the nastiest look on his face and snapped it off. In great disgust, he turned around and shook his finger at me.

"Daddy!" he scolded. "We *don't* watch TV with *niggers* on it in the house!"

I sat back on my chair and laughed, a big belly laugh, and put my feet up on the table. I was so PROUD! I thought, *Yeah, there's my son, the little Aryan son of a gun, my little man . . .*

As soon as that thought had passed, however, I thought, *Holy shit, Tommy, you're only three years old. What are you going to be like when you're fourteen?*

Suddenly my feet came off the table as quickly as I had put them up there. I did not like the thoughts running through my head. Flashback after flashback, scene after scene whizzed through my mind. Since the age of fourteen, I had been a fierce and reckless warrior, filled with the energy of hate. I thought about the fact that I had been arrested *sixteen times*. I thought about how fortunate I was not to be locked up in a federal penitentiary with the key thrown away—and I also knew the probability of my sons being that lucky was slightly less than zero. Cops were getting smarter. Hate crime bills and sentences were much harsher. Eventually people just go *down*. My cousin Johnny was sentenced to life in prison in San Quentin where he stayed until his death. I found myself seriously questioning where Tommy would be by the time he was fourteen—particularly seeing that he was already like this now. I began to wonder what he really had to look forward to in his life. Would there be life? Or was I leading him to his death?

Wham! It hit me between the eyes. Like my father before me, I had a double standard about my behavior. *My* involvement in the Movement was perfectly acceptable, but I didn't want my children to do this. I wanted my children to be something more than what I was. I didn't want them to be ignorant, tattooed racists. I wanted them to be presidents and senators and everything else caring parents genuinely want for their kids. If they followed my path, there was no way they would ever be successful. They would end up dead, in jail, or bombing Federal buildings.

I looked at my child, Tommy, who was sweet and pure and the light of my life. My eyes became opened to the innocence I had stolen from him, and that I was doing the same to Konrad. Over the next several months, I began to fiercely question my deepest-rooted beliefs and values.

A CHANGE IN PLANS

I threw a party in March of 1995 and invited Jesse, Sam, and Don. They were new friends who were Skinhead leaders from Idaho. Marty and the rest of my close friends came up to my house, but later I found out that Frank Tocash and a group of Skins went to another house to party, even though it was close by. Frank was in the Hammerskin leadership in San Diego. They were partying elsewhere because Frank and his boys were full-on potheads. They didn't want to be with us "clean Skins." We showed up at their party anyway. Jesse came with us, and he played it up with us, although the truth was that he was also a pothead.

Frank and the others tried to throw their weight around as soon as we got there. They were talking as if we had no authority to be there—that we had no authority at all. They were beyond wasted.

"You're a Skin, man!" I exclaimed to Frank, entirely disgusted. "You can't do dope."

"I can do whatever the hell I want," he sneered.

"Great," I countered. "Let's call Liz [Tarrant], and tell her you're all doing drugs. DON'T YOU GET IT? We're supposed to stay away from drugs, you freakin' idiots. We're supposed to be ELITE!" I wasn't just angry at these guys—I was angry at what was becoming so predominant among the Skins. "You guys make me sick."

I left with Marty and Jesse and Sam. I knew the guys at the party all started talking trash about me after we left. Back at my own party, I got falling-down drunk. I was no better off than Frank, but I was itching for a fight. My friends knew me well enough to sense my murderous intent.

"If you go back," Marty said, "we'll all go back to jail." He laughed. "I don't want to be taking long showers with you." We were being typical dumb guys, but the humor helped to diffuse my anger and the situation for a while. I forgot about Frank and turned my attention to the party. In the midst of my drunken condition, I started talking about the girls at my house. Marty was going on and on about the best-looking girl at the party.

"Yeah, Chris is a knockout," I agreed carelessly. "I should have been writing to her from Hawaii when I had the chance. If I had to do it all again, I would have gone for her instead of Nicole."

The next day, Marty said, "You know Nicole heard you last night, don't you?

"Heard what?" I asked. I was so hung over that I didn't remember much of anything, much less the conversation he and I had entertained about the girls the night before. It was stupid and although honest, it hurt Nicole's feelings. I felt bad that I had said something so unkind, and it caused Nicole to make some decisions I'm not sure she would have made if I wouldn't have said it in the first place.

Sam told me his group was going to Aryan Nations in April. It fell on a date close to Nicole's birthday and encompassed the entire weekend. It sounded intriguing to me. I needed new inspiration to get going. I needed something, anything to put my fire, my passion, into.

"How's the work up there, Sam?" I asked. I was in the process of selling the company with my dad, and I was going to get my cut. Sam and I talked for a bit about opportunities in Idaho. Later, Nicole said she wanted to go to Aryan Nations for her birthday present. What I didn't realize at the time was that she really wanted to meet Jesse. A few days later, I got an enlightening phone call from Jesse's wife.

"Did you know that when Jesse was down there at your place, he was having an affair with your wife?" she said. That hit hard. I had no idea.

"No, I didn't know that," I said, a little in shock.

"I think it's only fair that I tell you. Jesse and I are trying to work things out. I would appreciate it if you would make sure Nicole stays out of it."

I didn't tell Nicole about the phone call, and Jesse's wife didn't tell him she had called me. I also didn't tell Nicole that Jesse was too nervous to go to Aryan Nations anymore . . . let's just say people had been known to disappear from the compound, and he had made too many enemies now to be safe.

I told Nicole that if we were still going to Idaho for Aryan Nations, I wanted to attend the weekend as a family. I felt bad about what had happened between us and I honestly wanted to make it work with her. I drove the truck up a few days early to look for work. I spent most of my time with Sam and only ran into Jesse once. He still didn't know that I knew of his affair with my wife, and I didn't bring it up, although it was hard for both of us. He was nervous and I was cold. I spent time putting in resumes and applications where I could. Nicole flew up and brought the boys on Thursday, right before the weekend's festivities. I picked her up at the airport, and it wasn't until then that I let her know Jesse wasn't coming.

The gathering at Aryan Nations was huge. There were at least five to six hundred people at the compound. It was amazing to see racists and Skinheads who had come in from all over the nation. I was amazed and happy about it. Maybe things were not as bad as I thought they were. I got to hear Pastor Butler of Aryan Nations speak that weekend, and I attended two swastika burnings. I also met Buford Furrow. We were walking the grounds when I noticed Furrow's military tarp spread out on the lawn in front of the main house of the compound. This guy was talking to everyone about the gear he had laid out on the tarp, and discussing hand-to-hand combat. He was in the Army, so as a competitive ex-Marine I wanted to hear what he had to say.

"When the shit hits the fan," he said, his face serious, "and you got Feds and ZOGs coming after you, you'll need to survive in the field and the forest. You'll need to bring a propane stove." I started laughing at him.

"That's right," I joked. "In the middle of combat, just put explosives on your back!" He looked at me like I was the idiot, and I decided to expound a little to him and to the crowd.

"If you're really going to need something to burn in the wilderness," I explained, "pack a jar of peanut butter. It will burn ten times longer and it's not explosive." People nodded, seeing the sense in it. Buford didn't like me too much, needless to say, especially when I told him he needed to get more into survival techniques.

"I know what the hell I'm doing!" he barked. "I'm part of the security here at Aryan Nations." That's when I *knew* we were in trouble. Buford Furrow later furthered his "illustrious career" when he walked into a Jewish daycare center in Northridge, California, and shot five people, four of which were children.

Tommy, Konrad, and I were spending all of our time together because Nicole was with Dawn and Sam Dickie. I found out they were drinking inside the Aryan Nations compound, which was strictly against the rules. There were always big drinking parties later in the evenings right off the compound, but Dawn and Nicole wouldn't have been able to go.

"This sucks!" said Dawn. "Why did we bring the kids anyway? Now we can't go to any of the parties!" Her face was sour and I wished my boys and her kids hadn't heard her. I didn't think it was a good idea to go to the drinking festivities, anyway. From what I could see, people had already started getting stupid.

When we arrived on Saturday, we found out that the night before the band *Odin's Law* got so hammered they smashed up their hotel room. It cost Aryan Nations $1,200 to fix the damage so they wouldn't go to jail. Pastor Butler told everyone on Saturday that this wasn't an example of good or righteous behavior. I looked around, seeing that people didn't care what he was saying. They were snickering, winking, and being what I felt was disrespectful. Maybe that was always the moral fiber of Skins and racists, and I just hadn't noticed before.

All around me I saw backbiting, backstabbing, and total disregard for the rules. I realized I had been really selfish for a long time, just like these idiots. As long as something was good for me, then everything was good, but if it got in my way, it wasn't okay. The fact of the matter is, I was growing up, and I was thinking of other people and their rights and their feelings. I was especially thinking of my children. I didn't like how people were treating them, I didn't like the things they said around them, and I didn't like what they were learning. At one of the swastika burnings, we had taken a picture of Tommy giving the seig heil. I couldn't help but feel mixed emotions about the whole thing.

After we came back to California, Nicole and I were not getting along at all. I could tell it was just a matter of time before we split up. Every little thing was creating fights, and the hardest thing to swallow was that there was absolutely no respect between us. I had seen what that lack of respect did to couples and especially to the kids. I felt intense rage at myself and my situation, because I was following in the very footsteps of my father— something I swore I would never do. Something had to change.

My father and I sold our business and I got my share. Nicole and I were seriously considering moving up to Idaho, despite the threat of Jesse. I realized by then if she wanted to continue her affair or have another one,

I couldn't stop her. For a while, I had felt a jealous rage burning every time I thought of them together. After a while, I didn't care anymore. I just wanted things to work out for the sake of the kids. She was still their mother and would always be so. I felt it was better for them to be with their mom and dad despite the obstacles we were facing. I felt sad but resigned to the fact that there was no love in our marriage. There never really had been.

STIRRING UP HATRED

In June, I acquired a couple of big, money-making phone installations in Los Angeles as a side job. One day I was headed up to Banning to do a job, and I thought I would stop by and see my old friend Regina. I was headed in that direction anyway, and it had been a long time since we had connected. We had always been good friends but had been out of touch for quite some time since the many parties and get-togethers the BBB and American Firm had had at her house in Yucaipa. I had no idea what she was doing now.

Driving into Banning, I decided to visit the pawn shop her parents ran there and see how I could get in touch with her. It was strange to see the lights off and door shut, so I parked at the little gas station next door and walked around the corner. The first thing I saw was the closed sign. Maybe they were away on vacation. Then I saw a poster stapled to the front door. It had a picture of Regina on it. As I started reading it, my body went cold. I couldn't believe it. Surely this couldn't be right.

The poster read that the pawn shop had been robbed and that Regina had been murdered in the process. There was a number to call if anyone had information to give. I pulled the number off the poster and walked to my truck, where I sat in shock and actually called the police.

"Hey, I knew this girl that was killed at the pawn shop. Do you have any leads?" First, the officer took down my name and related information and how I knew Regina. Then he said the intruders had broken into the pawn shop to steal guns, and Regina had gotten in the way. They believed the robbery and murder was related to a couple of Mexican gangs in San Diego area. That's all they knew.

"Well, if I get any information," I lied, "I'll let you know." My shock had turned to anger in an instant, and I had murderous thoughts running through my head. The policeman had mentioned it was most likely a group of illegals. There were more cross-border gangs in that area than

I could count. Despite the mixed emotions I had been feeling about the racist movement, this murder of my dear friend, who was not involved in any kind of gang—she loved everybody—reinforced my ideas of hate and separatism. I felt at that moment if the world was all white, this wouldn't have happened. Beautiful Regina would still be running around.

I didn't want to think that whites would ever do this to her. I knew there were white serial killers. Ted Bundy was a freaking pervert—but of course I thought it was Jewish pornography that got him twisted. *Everything* that went bad was Jewish-controlled. Whenever a white guy went bad, I looked for evidence that it was due to our Jewish-controlled society, Jewish television and media. Besides, if America was an all-white country, we would just kill the freakin' idiots, and it wouldn't be a big deal. Whites killing whites most often didn't even make the news. My heart burned with that anger for a long time. I told my old buddies and they were as devastated and full of rage as I was. We never found out any additional information. That was fortunate for the people who committed the crime, or they would not still be alive.

I began driving into LA a couple of times a week with another Skin who would assist me with phone installations. Our jobs were all over, so we stopped in several different places to get lunch. One day we stopped at a fast food restaurant near one of the jobs, where we met a girl named Brooke from La Crescenta. We started talking and she was obviously flirting outrageously with me. My friend kept heckling me about it. I told her we'd probably be back there in a couple of days for another job. When we came back, she was there, waiting for us—waiting for me. Nicole and I hadn't been intimate in months, and somehow after her affair with Jesse, it didn't seem like a big deal. I ended up hooking up with Brooke. That affair lasted about two months.

Shortly thereafter, in August of 1995, Nicole and I finally made the decision to move to Idaho to become members of Hammerskin Nation in Idaho. Of all the places we looked at, we both thought Idaho would make all the difference in the world to our relationship. I honestly hoped it would be a new start for us. I was ready for a genuinely new beginning. I moved up there first, staying with Sam and Dawn in Hailey, Idaho. Housing was scarce. Initially we found a very small place and were relieved when we could move into a nice three-room house.

THE DOWNWARD SPIRAL OF HATE

Nicole began working nights at McDonald's. After a while, she started staying out until two or three in the morning. Jesse lived in the area and they were in contact with each other. I don't know if they were romantically involved or not. I never had proof—just the feeling that something wasn't right. Despite the change, and despite trying to reconcile things between us, we were both unhappy. As to our dreams in the Movement, everyone in California and Idaho assured me that the people I would be dealing with in Idaho were NOT druggies. Unfortunately, they were wrong again.

Jesse West was one of the leaders of the Movement in Idaho. I had an inkling that he was doing drugs, but it turned out he was a bigger doper than Johnny Bangerter. I wouldn't have known that was possible, but little by little, all the evidence revealed itself, and once again I felt trapped and furious. Once again I had been promised a "down white man" who was nothing but a dope and meth addict. Because of this, we would spend less than eight months in Idaho. However, the events that took place there affected me and my children forever.

As time passed, all Nicole and I did was work and come home and go back to work. The Movement was practically non-existent. There simply was no activity in that neck of the woods. There were only five of us until another guy moved in. What's amazing to me was that up there in the boonies, a serious division existed within that tiny racist cell. Me and a couple of other guys didn't want any part of Jesse or his drug habits. I had to accept that what was happening here mirrored the Movement across the nation, but it still infuriated me. To me it was personal. I felt like they were tarnishing the reputation of *my* Skins.

"If Jesse wants to call himself a Peckerwood, that's one thing," I argued. "That's what he is." Peckerwoods were Skins notorious for their drugs. As a recruiter, however, I sure as hell didn't want other kids to come into the Movement calling themselves a member of Hammerskin Nation and seeing him as an example. The problems I encountered in Utah, California, and Idaho were never resolved.

The polarization happening between clean and dirty white supremacists—and between clean and dirty Skins—was all coming to a head. I not only witnessed but became embroiled in all the sick and twisted political games taking place. I was sick of the hypocrisy. I was actually sick of the whole Movement.

Unbeknownst to any of my fellow Skins, I felt drawn to talk to other people—people outside the Movement. I started having discussions with many different people, from different religions, backgrounds, and ethnic groups (well, as many as you can get in Idaho, anyway).

One day I ran into a black man and his little girls when I was out on a job by myself. I could tell he wasn't from around there. We both noticed each other's tattoos, yet we had a frank conversation.

"Why did you move *here*?" I asked him. I was intrigued and I really wanted to know.

"I had to get my daughters away from the kids in our old neighborhood," he said. "The drugs, the violence—it was no way for me to raise my girls. I did what I had to do to survive, but as a dad, I wanted to make sure that they weren't forced to make the same choices." I nodded. My boys weren't even in school yet, but I knew exactly what he was talking about.

I talked to a Hispanic guy who was almost sleeved in ink. He had gotten into a lot of trouble too, and had moved to Idaho for the same reason: to take care of his family and get them away from all the dangers in his old neighborhood. I kept running into people like this and talking to them about all number of things, from life choices to religion and philosophies. I had to be very, very careful, though, and not let my buddies see these interactions. It would have raised too many questions I wasn't prepared to answer yet.

At the time I was working for GJ Farrington in Sun Valley. I had started working with Jesse and Sam, but issues between Jesse and I escalated until he took off to start his own thing, and I only had to work with Sam. I was looking for something better and started doing electrical work, installing house and phone jobs, and so forth. Although things weren't so great between Nicole and myself, I kept working at it. I believed it was the best thing for everyone involved. Still, it seemed every day was tougher to take.

One of the biggest fights Nicole and I ever got into was actually over the police. We had been out together and Tommy saw a policeman. Nicole turned to him.

"Those are ZOG Stormtroopers," she told Tommy and Konrad. "They are the *enemy*! Stay away from them because they are evil."

I stopped for a second in shock and turned to her. She wasn't saying anything that I hadn't heard a thousand times before, and even believed in to a point, but this was going too far.

"Never tell that to our boys again, do you hear me?" I demanded. "What if some crazy child molester was trying to kidnap them? Or some other jerk? They would *need* to go to the police for help and would be too frightened to do it! They could be kidnapped or killed, just because you're going to make them too afraid to go for help!"

"You are supporting the ZOGs again!" she screamed. "It's all because of your brother Phil, isn't it?" It was true that I didn't want my children to be frightened of or to hate my brother Phil. He was now working for Rialto Police Department and had married a Hispanic cop, which solidified his evil, race traitorous, Zionistic status in Nicole's eyes. I loved my brother Phil, my sister-in-law, and my kids enough that I thought some of this ZOG Stormtrooper stuff was pure bullshit. I had gotten to know a lot of police officers and sheriffs in my day, and some of them were not half bad—even when I was acting like an idiot. While I admit some were real jerks, usually they were just doing their jobs. Sometimes people, including Nicole, took propaganda too far. I had used it for my own purposes and twisted it around whenever I needed to push something or rationalize one of my actions to others. However, I felt like I could separate truth from fervor, and I felt like she couldn't.

In April of 1996 we journeyed up to Aryan Nations again for Nicole's birthday weekend. It was Hitler's birthday celebration, too. Nicole was always proud that her birthday was one day before his. The whole dynamics at Aryan Nations was different than the previous year. Less than half the number of people attended, perhaps only two hundred. In addition, it seemed to me that everyone present that year looked like trash, especially the group of Skins that Nicole was hanging out with. They had big egos and kept having to prove themselves in a violent manner to everyone around them. I saw them beat up some random guy over a pack of cigarettes. Whatever respect I might have had for them simply because of the brotherhood was lost at that point. I was hanging out with a pretty clean group from Memphis that I felt more comfortable with. The two groups clashed miserably.

That weekend I was excited to attend one of Pastor Richard Butler's little get-togethers at the church. White supremacists from around the nation were meeting to discuss several issues, including the government's conspiracy against us, the threat of the United Nations and World Bank, successful recruiting techniques, the latest on weapons, and Aryan unity.

I had come to several of these types of leadership meetings in past years. In attendance, as usual, were other Skinheads from around the nation, neo-Nazis, and Aryan brothers. There were also a bunch of ex-convicts and white brothers who simply hated everyone else, hated the government, and wanted to do something about it.

This time, I had some things that had been bothering me. I was in leadership, and a lot of people listened to what I had to say. In the middle of a meeting, I stood up and asked a perfectly reasonable question.

"What happens when we've killed off all the Jews and the blacks and the Hispanics and it's just us?" I asked. "What then?"

"Sit down and shut up, TJ!" snarled some idiot sitting nearby. "Because we'll start with hair color next." People broke out into laughter, but I wanted a real answer.

"No, come on, really. Let's have a serious discussion about this." Again, I got the same brainless response. "We'll start to get rid of frea-kin' redheads like you!" they laughed. We all laughed our asses off . . . but somewhere within the laughter the lack of answers made me real-ize that the Movement wasn't really about white power. It was simply about *hatred*. Once we'd annihilated everyone else, once there were only whites, we would turn on ourselves. And it wouldn't matter—starting with whomever—the redheaded guys or the brown-eyed people, or the short ones, or whatever . . . it didn't matter, we would destroy ourselves, one by one.

It was all about hate, hate, hate. It didn't have anything to do with truth, or even cleansing, because it would *never* stop. What we were talk-ing about here, what I had been teaching, spouting, and spewing for all of my adult life was annihilation through ignorant hatred. For the first time, I wasn't sure there would be anybody left.

I looked around me and realized I didn't want any part of this. I didn't want to preach it, to push it, and I certainly didn't want to live it.

Just a few days later, on April 26, 1996, I left the Movement.

15

NATURE VERSUS NURTURE

I'M ASHAMED TO admit that from the time of my epiphany with Tommy and Konrad and *Gullah, Gullah Island* until the day I left the Movement, it took me a good eighteen months to decide to fully break out. For a while I felt like I absolutely had no choice, but my final decision was based on many factors. First, I wasn't getting answers to my questions about the Movement's value system and goals. In addition, I was finally growing up and realizing that this cause I had been living for was a farce. More deeply than that, I had seen evidence it was adversely affecting my children. It may be one thing to live in the crap of my own making, but it was quite another to realize I was forcing it onto my own children and driving them into a life of hate.

Once I was sure I was leaving, my mind was made up. I was DONE, determined to walk away and never look back. I curiously found myself as passionate about letting go as I had been earlier about embracing it. I didn't tell anyone else, but I told Nicole. I told her about my feelings, my disillusionment, and how I wanted to break out and away, forever. Unfortunately, Nicole didn't feel the same way. When I asked her to leave the Movement with me, she refused.

"I believe in the cause!" she yelled at me angrily. "And I think you are weak and irrational! By leaving the Movement, you are betraying me, you're betraying the kids, and you are betraying the Movement. I *will* raise these boys in the truth of the Movement. I will raise them to be what they deserve—racists and separatists—and you cannot stop me."

This scene was the final straw in our relationship. We had never been close, piecing together a relationship that had been brought together by hate and not real love. Without the Movement, we didn't have a single other thing in common except the kids. For the next few days, we barely tolerated each other. Nicole wouldn't speak to me except a word here or there. One night when the boys were in bed, we were watching TV. I wanted to talk it out.

"What's going on?" I finally asked Nicole. "We're not a couple, we're not together. We're nothing."

"What's going on," she said, "is that I don't think I love you."

I wasn't hurt so much by her comment as by the reality of the situation. I had been trying so hard to make the family work. I had been busting my butt to make everyone happy, and she and I were both miserable. It was time to split up. I knew there were a lot of opportunities in New Mexico for telecommunications. I said I would go there the next morning.

"When I get settled," I said glumly, "I'll bring you and the kids down and we'll get everyone financially settled to where we can file for divorce."

"No!" Nicole said adamantly. "No, we'll just split up, separate, and see how it goes." For some reason, that didn't sit well with me. Emotionally, we'd already been living that way from almost the beginning. It was sheer hell, and it wasn't good for the kids. I remembered all the trauma I'd experienced as a kid—the jealous rages, the abuse, the fighting, the embarrassment. I would not put my kids through that.

"Look," I said. "This doesn't work. When you sleep with whomever and I sleep with whomever—it just confuses the heck out of the kids."

Nicole just looked at me. There was no emotion in her eyes. "Well, you need to know I'm going up to Washington."

"Washington? What are you going to do there?"

"My new friends from there—the Skin group you met at Aryan Nations—they've formed a society in Washington. The boys and I will go there."

I wanted Nicole to be happy, and I knew I wasn't in control of what she did. However, as much as I witnessed at Aryan Nations, I sure didn't want those guys around my kids.

"All the drugs and crap that group is into, are you kidding? You can't take the boys up there in that mess!"

"It's too late," she said. "They're getting ready to come and get me and the boys."

"The hell they are!" I ranted. "You can't do this to the boys, Nicole! These guys are potheads and methheads. Surely you can see that?"

She just shook her head. I found out the number and called the lead Skin in Washington.

"You had better not come down here or I will kill you. Are you clear?" He was. He knew my reputation, and he wasn't about to mess with me.

The next day I left for New Mexico to look for work. By the following day, I had an incredible offer from a telecommunications company, for more money than the two of us had ever made together. I called Nicole right away.

"Why don't you bring the kids down here? We'll get divorced, but we can both be here for the kids." Nicole had other plans.

"They're coming to get me," she said, speaking of the Washington Skins. I was furious.

For the second time I called leadership in Washington and I warned them. "You come get her, and I'll kill all of you and your friends." They backed down. At the same time, I'm thinking, *Is this what life is all about? There has to be something more—something better, something less insane, healthier, and happier. There has to be a better answer for the boys.* Deep in my heart, when I had the courage to go there, something else spoke to me. Something else was calling me to something cleaner, more real, and truer than what I had been living and thinking all of my life. But what?

Nicole called me back.

"Please let them come and get me, TJ," she pleaded. "Please let me go up there with them. I know you don't like them, but it won't be that bad."

"Let me think about it," I said. "I'll call you back." I got in the truck and drove straight to California. I didn't even know why I was driving there. Thoughts battled inside my brain. I knew I was done with the Movement. Done. It was all so insane, so bizarre. I had another experience of all my memories flooding back—the lies, the violence, the hatred, the insanity of it all. It was all I could do to make it to where my mother was living, with my brother Mat. I only stopped for gas, not to eat or drink or anything. I had to get there as fast as I could.

Getting out of the truck, I practically ran to the door and began knocking. When my mother opened the door, she was shocked to see me standing there.

"TJ, what are you doing here?" she cried, and threw her arms around me. "Are you okay? What's going on?" I looked her in the eyes and told her what she'd been waiting over a decade to hear.

"I left the Movement, Mom." She gasped, and I continued. "I completely walked away from it. Nicole still believes in it and she won't leave. She's wanting to go up to Washington to live in some freaking drug compound with the boys. We're getting a divorce."

My mother was elated that I was leaving the Movement. I think she was happy that Nicole and I were splitting up because she knew she wasn't good for me, but she didn't mention her. I had never seen my mother be unkind to a soul in my life.

"Thank goodness you are getting out of that Movement!" she exclaimed. "But what about Tommy and Konrad? You can't just leave them to rot in that place, can you? They'll . . . They'll end up . . ."

"Like me. Yes, I know. They'll end up like me or worse." I knew exactly what my mother meant, and for the first time, I really saw and felt what she had been through, having me as her son. I was awash in emotion. How could I let Nicole take my boys up to Washington to live, to grow up amidst that group? Just like the morning my boys and I watched *Gullah Gullah Island* together, I knew the fate they were destined for if someone didn't intervene. Tommy and Konrad, who saluted Nazi flags and Hitler, who dressed so proudly in braces and fatigues, who only knew the crap that we had taught them—I couldn't leave them to die in that place. If I didn't get them out of the Movement, they would be raised in it until they were adults (if they made it that far), and they would know only hate and nothing else. I *had* known something better, only I had walked away from it in my anger and rage. I had made a mess of my own life, but my sons wouldn't have even a sliver of hope unless I had the courage to do something.

I called Nicole right away.

"I'm in California, Nicole," I said. She was surprised, and I continued. "I've thought a lot about our situation. Please come back with me to California. I'll get you a place of your own to live in, and I'll pay for it. I'll grant you a divorce so you can live your own life, but this way we can both be an integral part of the kids' lives."

"No," she said.

"Please, Nicole," I begged her. "I'm out of the Movement because it's immature; it's sick and wrong—like these guys that beat people up for cigarette money. Please do this for me. And if you can't do it for me, do it for the kids, and for yourself. You don't have to live with a bunch of doped up guys."

"No," she said. "I don't care that you don't like these guys. I'm taking the kids, and we're moving to Washington." Nothing I could say would sway her. She wouldn't listen to my worries about the children, she wouldn't listen to anything derogatory about the Movement. I was starting to panic. Once she moved to Washington, I would have no recourse to see my kids. The faces of my children swam in front of me . . . my sweet innocent kids. They would be raised every day around drugs, sex, violence, and hatred for all other people, and eventually themselves. Once Tommy and Konrad were up there, especially because I had admitted I was leaving the Movement, the Skins would probably never let me see my kids again. They might even kill me if I tried, and all the Skins would laugh and say, "Good riddance!"

At first, all kinds of murderous thoughts went through my mind. After so many years of living this way, it was taking time to disentangle my thought processes from my violent behavior. My friends in California didn't know I had left the Movement. My friends in Oregon, Texas, and so forth didn't know either. People were known to mysteriously disappear on the road from one state to another. Other strategies played themselves out in my mind, but I couldn't wrap my arms around any of them. In the last eighteen months, my heart had melted, my intellect had opened, and I wasn't capable of the things I once was. For one thing, I loved my sons so much, I could never take their mother from them. While it was easier to think of knocking off the Skins from Washington, curiously enough, I couldn't do that, either. I was determined to step away from the Movement entirely, and that also meant the life of violence I had embraced for so long. I wanted to be the kind of dad my kids could look up to. I couldn't do anything about my stupid past, but I could start this minute to do only the things that I believed in, from the heart.

Even though I had just arrived in California an hour or two earlier, from there I drove straight up to Idaho and didn't stop to rest once. I had a sense of compelling urgency. This wasn't about me or Nicole anymore. It had everything to do with the kids. I arrived quite early in the morning and knocked on the door. Just like my mother a few hours before, Nicole was surprised to see me. She could tell I was exhausted.

"Can I sleep on the couch?" I asked, honoring her feelings for physical separation. I also knew she was uncomfortable with me being there, because she was afraid I was going to hurt or kill the guys coming to get her. After all, I had threatened their lives.

"Nicole, I'm not going to hurt your friends," I said, wanting to reassure her. "I just came to get my stuff. You have every right to go with them if you want to."

She looked relieved, though still unsure. "They'll be here sometime late tomorrow."

I nodded, then headed for the couch, where I slept hard and didn't wake up until the next day when Nicole began packing up. The boys and I were happy to see each other, and we played for a bit. I tried to be casual, but my brain was in overdrive. The Washington Skins were on their way, and I knew they would be armed to the teeth, especially because they were preparing to deal with me. My kids were in grave danger, and it was quite possible we would never see each other again. I wasn't the only Skin who knew how to make people disappear. Still, I wasn't so scared for me as I was for them. I wondered how in the world I could get Nicole to let me have the kids for a while, and for the first time since I was a young boy, I began to pray.

Nicole announced she had gotten money from her aunt to lease a U-haul truck, so I drove her down to pick it up. While we were driving back to her place, I noticed there was a carnival in town. Back at our place, I started helping Nicole get things loaded up, when her friends arrived much earlier than she had expected (or at least much earlier than she had told me). They weren't being aggressive with me, yet. I had to think quickly.

"Remember that carnival that we saw on the way over here?" I asked Nicole. "I'd like to take the boys over to it and spend a little time before they have to go." She agreed. She had her hands full getting everything loaded up.

An hour and a half later, I called her from Jackpot, Nevada. I told her I was on my way to California where I would file for divorce.

"Don't you take my boys away from me!" she yelled. She had a right to be upset, just as I did that she wanted to take them away from me to Washington.

"I'm not going to have the boys raised with a bunch of freakin' drugged-up idiots," I said. It wasn't a good situation, and I wished it could have been better—for all of us. Still, I knew the consequences of not taking a stand for my boys. I knew in my gut that this was a critical juncture. I let Nicole talk to the boys and she told them she missed them and that she would see them soon. I understood how she felt and I had no intention of separating the boys from their mother indefinitely. I just hoped she would come to her senses about the Washington compound. She never would, until the court forced her to.

Nicole ended up moving to Longview, Washington, where I sent her divorce papers. The gang of Skinheads she lived with was trying to organize themselves into some kind of communal system. They were all about her age or younger, and I think she liked one of the guys, but I really didn't have proof. Honestly, that part didn't bother me because I wanted her to be happy. What bothered me were the drugs and the lifestyle. My fears about the compound were truer than I initially thought. From my contact with them at Aryan Nations, I knew the whole group took drugs, but I didn't know that they were manufacturing them as well. Several months down the road, these Skins got busted for operating a methamphetamine lab. In the meantime, however, Nicole got their support, their money, and a lawyer. I didn't have one.

The long, ugly battle for custody was just beginning.

16

CLEANSING ETHNIC HATRED

MY HEART WAS filled with so much anger my first several months back in California. I felt lost, knowing I had wasted my life away in the Movement. I didn't have a cause, I didn't have a focus, and I had no idea which direction I was going to turn. I had been a Skin for so many years, and quite suddenly my identity was completely gone. I was still ready to fight—but it was for a different battle now. Nicole was trying to get my boys back. While all my bridges to the past had been burned, it's a good thing that at the time I didn't know how hot those fires would become.

My mother continued to be joyously happy, however, that I was leaving my old ways behind. She had always believed that this obsession of mine wasn't really the true me—that I couldn't really believe all that neo-Nazi propaganda. I knew she had been in denial, but Mom looked at it a different way. She said she had continued to have faith in God and never let go of the hope that I could change. I was doing my best. I severed all ties with any Skins. No one knew where to find me, and I was okay with that. I went to live with Mat until I got my own apartment, and I started working for my dad on a job up in the high desert. I had a lot of time to think on the way to and from work.

In the meantime, Nicole was making life hell. One morning I was served the child custody paperwork. My family and I were desperate to keep the kids, and we were angry at her for thinking she deserved them in the lifestyle she wanted to raise them in. Although she was still living in the Washington area with white supremacists in a violent, neo-Nazi environment, the court still wanted to give her the legal rights to take the kids back to live with her. I was beside myself with anger and grief. When I had taken the kids from her, all I wanted was to protect them from the Movement and the crazy people in it, but I didn't feel like the court had a clue. I knew first-hand what Skins were like and what they were capable of. How could I possibly let my kids be raised in that harsh environment?

Nicole was able to get an ex parte hearing for June 5, 1996. Her lawyer brought up the fact that I had kidnapped the children and therefore violated her rights. I explained to the judge that she was still heavily involved in the Movement and I had completely left it because of the immediate and long-term danger to my children. The judge said that just because *I* had admitted to having been involved with the Movement, it didn't mean she was, and it didn't prove that the kids were in danger.

"Even if the kids were kidnapped so they didn't have to live with felons and thugs?" I asked.

"Is that true?" the judge asked. Nicole denied it, and he told me that I had to take the kids to Washington.

One morning I went to my mother to talk about the custody papers I had been served. I could tell the judge didn't care what Nicole was involved in, and he didn't believe that I had walked away from the Movement. I had deliberately severed *all* ties, all associations (except to Nicole, for the sake of my sons). I wanted to know what I could legally do to keep my boys safe. I had begun a huge shift and was no longer operating from anger and vengeance like I had all my life. Still, it was frustrating. Nicole had an entire white power camp behind her and lots of money for lawyers. I had nothing, except my mother's prayers.

By this time, I had been out of the Movement for about two and a half months. That morning my mother had news and a challenge for me. She had watched a television program that had featured Rabbi Hier and the Simon Wiesenthal Center's Museum of Tolerance. She suggested I go and visit them. I looked at her and wondered what she'd been smoking.

"Mom, Jews don't exactly party with Skinheads on Friday and Saturday nights," I said.

Still, it was something to think about. Besides, I was a former Skinhead now, and I found out that the Simon Wiesenthal Center was actually an international Jewish human rights organization—obviously totally opposite than anything I'd ever dealt with before. Dedicated to preserving the memory of the Holocaust, the organization said it fostered tolerance and understanding through community involvement, educational outreach, and social action. Contemporary issues such as racism, anti-Semitism, terrorism, and genocide were all right up their educational alley. I got the idea that maybe someone at the museum could make use of all the racist junk I'd accumulated over the years. After I thought about it for a couple of days, I ended up calling them. The call was primarily to please my mother, and a symbol to her and to myself of really letting go of my past, my old beliefs, and my old way of life. I had no need for the junk anymore anyway. Maybe it would come to good use.

When I called, I told the operator at the center that I had loads of white power materials I would like to donate to the museum if they desired, and I asked if they could come and get it all. Obviously they didn't get calls like that every day. Finally they put me through to Richard Eaton, their senior researcher who had done some tremendous work involving Nazis and neo-Nazis in Germany. I talked to him for a few minutes on the phone and set an appointment to bring in the materials that I had. We both figured it would take about half an hour.

Rick's office was next door to the Museum of Tolerance and up on the second floor in a very tiny space he shared with Aaron Brightbart. Rick was probably six foot one, very thin, had a beard that matched his light brown, nearly blond hair that was sprinkled with a little gray. When I showed up at Rick's office, I think I floored him when I carried in my first large box and said there was more outside.

"Really?" he exclaimed. "Are you serious? There's more?" He came out with me to my truck and saw that my vehicle was stuffed with two file cabinets worth of documents, pictures, CDs, videos, and numerous racist flags; the accumulation of fifteen years of hate paraphernalia. When Rick saw all of this stuff, his eyes nearly popped out of his head. I saw the wheels turning in his head, but he played it casual. He had this incredibly funny sense of humor and started talking to me about some of the stuff he knew about the Movement.

"What do you think about John Metzger?" he asked me, referring to Tom Metzger's son, who was often seen at leadership meetings with his father and anything that had to do with Tom's *WAR* newspaper. "Do you know of him? Have you met him?"

"Well, yes, I have," I admitted. "To be quite honest with you, I think he's a closet homosexual. Not that anyone would dare be an open homosexual in the white power environment. Still, everyone I know that's met him thinks he probably is. John has kids, but not everyone knows that his kids are not from him."

Rick and Aaron kind of laughed at my comments, and we joked about some other things as well. Later on, Rick told me he knew that I knew what I was talking about when I spoke candidly about John. "Anybody that *really* knows anything about white power knows that," he said.

Suddenly Rick wanted to talk to me about everything, and about my involvement in the Movement, how I got out, and what I was doing now. Our "half an hour" ended up taking two and a half weeks!

The Wiesenthal Center had just done an investigation into the ties of neo-Nazis in Germany with neo-Nazis in the United States. They had infiltrated groups on both sides, and Rick was involved in things that were happening in Europe and the United States. Initially he was worried that I might be a spy. As we started talking and I blurted everything, he would be off on a few things here and there, and I would set him straight. Most of it was things he already knew. I didn't know he was testing me.

Rick and I had experienced many people who had planned to get out of gangs, but they usually got sucked right back in to their old life-style. Somehow Rick could tell I was the real thing—that I had been a Skinhead and a very powerful leader and that I had walked away for good. He sensed my sincerity that I was there to purge the past and move on. I was pretty pissed off about the place I was in and the choices that I made, and I knew there was no way in hell I was ever going back.

Rick informed Rabbi Abraham Cooper, Associate Dean of the Wiesenthal Center, about our talks. Rabbi Cooper called me ten days later and left a message asking me to meet with him and Rabbi Marvin Hier, the dean and founder of Wiesenthal Center. Reluctantly, I agreed, though I kept thinking, *Why? What the hell would these guys want with me?*

The thought of that meeting was terrifying to me. I was raised strictly Irish-Catholic. Before I joined the Skins I used to go see a priest every Wednesday to confess a week's worth of sins. *That* was bad enough! Now I was supposed to divulge fifteen years of sins to two Jewish rabbis? I was scared to death. I needed reinforcement. I decided to bring in my big guns—*my mommy!* It didn't matter that I was thirty years old, that I had committed a thousand crimes, that I had been able to do drive-bys without even shuddering; I wanted her by my side to help me through this.

The morning dawned, and Mom and I headed into LA and over to Pico Boulevard. The Museum of Tolerance stands kitty-corner across from the Simon Wiesenthal Center. I was quaking on the inside, but I had already resigned myself to the task. Maybe there was some good that could come out of all the crap I'd been through—all the hell I'd put other people through too.

We went up to the third floor for the interview, into a small conference room. There was a big square table, with chairs all the way around it. The walls showcased artwork from a woman who had created a lot of Holocaust paintings. There to meet us were Rabbi Hier, Rabbi Cooper, and a reporter from *Time* magazine. At first, I was petrified. Some deep part of me was very much afraid they weren't going to believe me, or if they did believe me, they wouldn't understand why I was dong this. *I* wasn't even sure why I was doing this, and I certainly didn't understand why they wanted to talk to me. I remember having paranoid thoughts from all my years of indoctrination. I was afraid they were going to want to probe me.

Rabbi Cooper spoke first. He was five foot eight, a little stocky, with a full salt and pepper beard and mustache—very Orthodox, from his glasses to his clothing. He was very impressive and unconsciously intimidating, at least to me. Right away I could tell he was very intelligent and also extremely well-spoken in a fatherly, though undeniably powerful, sort of way.

Rabbi Marvin Hier seemed a little less intimidating. Dressed in a business suit and tie, he was a rather unorthodox, Orthodox Jew. At five foot six, he also wore glasses, but smaller ones. Unlike Rabbi Cooper, he had no facial hair. He was quieter than Rabbi Cooper and stayed in the background, content to listen or to ask only specific questions. (I found out later how unconvinced he really was. In a television interview he said, "My reaction to TJ was that I was skeptical as can be. *Come on, he probably just wants to infiltrate us—he's going to use us.* When I saw him for the first time, tattoos and all, believe me, it didn't change my mind that easily!")

One of the major questions they asked was why I had come to the museum. I was honest. I told them I hadn't really wanted to come—but that since I was turning my back on the Movement for good, my mom suggested that I bring all the hate paraphernalia I had so that something good might actually come out of it. It was this relationship with my mother that began to sway them to see that I was telling the truth—that I was authentic in my desire to shed my old life. "I saw the relationship," admitted Rabbi Hier. "I couldn't believe that anyone who had that kind of relationship with his mother was capable of using her for some kind of scheme."

He was right. While I had proven I was capable of very harsh things, I wasn't capable of *that*. It was my mother who told me she would walk beside me whenever I decided to leave the Movement. She had supported my higher self for as long as I could remember, and I respected and loved her for that. Rabbi Hier also saw my concern for the way I was raising my children.

"All the hatred I spent all my time perpetuating has been coming out in my oldest son—and is soon to show up in my baby boy too," I told him grimly. "The way I've been leading them, they won't end up as doctors finding a cure for cancer, or a judge on the Supreme Court. They'll be beating people up. They'll be spending time in jail. Worst of all, they'll be ignorant of any choices except being punk kids using hate to get what they want."

The rabbis were very interested in the goings on, the beliefs, and the recruitment tactics of Skinheads. They wanted to understand the Skins' involvement in Aryan Nations as well. They kept asking me questions about things they didn't know or fully grasp. I was amazed. Some of what we discussed they understood fairly clearly, and with the insight and some more background that I gave them, it clicked—they got it because of their knowledge and experience. In certain areas, however, they were completely off base.

For example, while the rabbis were extremely well-informed about many white power groups, when it came to the Skinhead Movement they were fairly ignorant of the beliefs and internal structure. I did my best to explain the difference. They thought the philosophy was still about loving America, embracing the flag, and wanting to keep it right-wing and white. I informed them that while in the beginning this had been the Skins' philosophy, it had changed drastically over the years. Most groups of Skins believed in destroying America and rebuilding it completely into what *they* wanted.

As far as the roles and the rulers, they did have the national names and people down pat. They had a fairly good grasp of the core beliefs of groups and their ideals—especially of the older racist groups. They were much less knowledgeable about the younger clans like the Peckerwoods and Skinheads. They didn't realize the politics, the history, or the games behind the scenes.

Several times, the conversation wound back to why I would be so willing to give them this information. Finally I said, "Well, I created this mess, and I feel like I have to clean it up. It's up to me take responsibility for what I've done, and I recognize that this is one way to do it. Then I can move on with my life." Despite my fear, the meeting actually went very well. Again we expected it to last one to two hours maximum, but we were all there from ten AM until six PM and had barely scratched the surface of what I could tell them when it was time to go.

Later my mom would tell me she just knew I was going to be okay after that meeting. In her own mind, she realized that perhaps I had to go through all that ugliness for so long, just so I could help people turn their own lives around. She saw a light turn on in me she hadn't seen for a long, long time. I think she saw a glimpse of a mission that neither I nor the rabbis had even thought of.

17

Fraternizing with the Enemy

APPARENTLY WHEN RICK first talked to the rabbis, they didn't think much would come of it. I'm sure they thought, *Ah, a Skinhead—he won't be able to put two sentences together* (except that being in their line of work, these guys really try not to stereotype). Rick told them I was intelligent, talkative, and that I could put things into perspective for other people. They began to see that, but they tested me. They grilled me, and scrutinized my reaction to everything they said. The rabbis ended up talking much more with me than I think they were initially prepared for. I was an anomaly. No one had ever come to them freely with so much information, and with the passion that I had. Internally, I was determined to purge everything, to somehow right some tremendous wrongs that I knew I was responsible for.

As much as I wanted to, there were times when it wasn't easy to divulge some of my deepest, darkest secrets to people I had honestly considered the enemy for so long. What got me to be more open and revealing were my easy conversations with Rick Eaton. It was actually warm and comfortable talking to him, very easy to tell him everything that had been going on. He had a great sense of humor, and he was very kind, even in the midst of some of the struggles I was having. He knew a lot about the Movement, so it was easy to talk to him, like to one of my old buddies. Initially, I didn't feel warmth or trust from anyone else at the Wiesenthal Center, and I couldn't blame any of them. I was grateful that when I talked to the rabbis, Rick was usually there. It calmed my nerves considerably.

The next few weeks went by in a blur. Some days we spoke for up to twelve hours. Some days I didn't come, busy with work and doing everything I could within the court system to get my boys back.

One day when I came in, I was totally unprepared for what Rabbi Cooper was about to ask me.

"Do you want to speak out?" he asked, his look piercing and serious. "Do you want to become involved with the Simon Wiesenthal Center?"

I don't know if I answered him right away; it set me back a little bit. In fact, it was kind of weird. During our conversations, there was a lot of growth that had happened. In spending so much time with the rabbis and discussing hate groups, I had overcome a lot of my beliefs and stereotypes I had harbored so long about Jews. What was shocking to me was when Rabbi Hier discussed with me hate groups that I never even knew existed.

"Everybody hates, TJ," Rabbi Hier had said to me. "There are white, black, and even Jewish hate groups." Wow! The fact that this rabbi was open and willing to admit to hate groups and factions within his own culture blew me away. It was not what I had pictured at all, especially through my indoctrinated beliefs. I thought Jews always stuck up for Jews—so why would he bring that out? A foundation of trust had been fostered between myself and the rabbis, and it had to do with both sides being intensely honest, no matter what that looked like. I had no idea how much trust had been built until the moment Rabbi Cooper asked me to speak out.

Whatever thought processes I had going on in my head at that moment, it only took seconds to realize that I really did have a strong desire to speak out. I was almost shocked with the realization. Still, I told the rabbis that I would like to talk it over with my family, because I was not the only one that would be affected. That night, my whole family got together for the first time in five years. Everyone except my father agreed whole-heartedly that it was the right thing to do. Only my father was against me speaking out, because he was worried about repercussions. I had to take a long hard look at that. Still, by the end of the night I was ready to do my part to stop the hate that I had helped to create.

When I told the rabbis of my decision, Rabbi Cooper was truly concerned for my safety. It was one thing to come clean, to purge secretly to them. It was another thing entirely to become the poster boy for annihilation.

I agreed to become a speaker for tolerance for the Simon Wiesenthal

Center on two conditions. The first was that the rabbis and I completely agreed that the Simon Wiesenthal Center could be in no way connected to my custody battle. I didn't want the Movement saying the Jews won my kids for me. I knew I had to do it on my own. It was time for me to stand up, to be the man I should have been long ago.

The second condition was that I be given the opportunity to speak to junior high and high school students, and as often as possible. There was a very personal reason for this. Kids ranging in age from eleven to eighteen years were the targeted audience that I had been recruiting for years, and they were exactly who was being targeted by the local Skinheads *at that minute*. If I was going to speak out, this was the ultimate audience with whom I was determined to make a positive difference.

18

180 Degrees—and Hotter

"ONCE I GO public," I told Rabbi Cooper simply, "life will change." That was a prophetic understatement.

On August 12, 1996, I did my first presentation at a junior high in Bakersfield, California—ironically my target recruiting audience for the Skins for the past fifteen years, but this was the first time I was motivating kids to stay *out* of gangs instead of inviting them in. The next day, August 13 (less than twenty-four hours later), there was an entire website devoted to my demise. Racist David Lynch, the Eastern states commander for the American Front, called me a "butt plug" among some choice expletives. Western Hammerskins wrote advice to others in the Movement to "terminate on sight." This website actually remained in the public domain until 2005, when some friends of mine at the FBI finally determined it was criminal and forced them to close it down. At the time, I chose not to worry too much about the threat. This was the name of the game. The opposition was just being predictable.

From experience I knew that gangs stayed tight for good reason. It was often a life-or-death situation if someone broke away, especially if they were going to be a snitch. I was more than a snitch—I was a great threat to the entire White Power Movement. I knew how the players thought, what they talked about, how they were recruiting, what their goals, plans, dreams, and games were. I knew how they operated. They wanted me dead.

My former best friend, Marty Cox, became a singer in a racist band called Extreme Hatred. His claim to fame was that he was on *Oprah* and he called Oprah Winfrey a monkey. After I left the Movement, Marty wrote a song about me, entitled "Race Traitor," with graphic and explicit lyrics about me and what I had done. He sang the song live a number of times in front of audiences, telling our story and calling me by name along with his more descriptive words. He continued to play in white power bands where he still sung that old, worn-out song about me.

Within a few weeks, I was interviewed for *Time* magazine, *48 Hours,* and the *LA Times.* I appeared on several radio programs, and life suddenly got crazier. I was used to people knowing who I was, but not to this kind of national scale. Rick Eaton accompanied me to these appearances across the United States and Canada, and I was glad to have someone who believed in me by my side. He was a real friend and an anchor, especially when I received hundreds of death threats every day. Rick was really worried about them, but I wasn't at first. They were your everyday, average death threats with very little creativity, full of epithets and vibrant language. "You race scum . . . I'm going to kill you . . . I'll kill your mother . . . Don't forget, I know exactly where you live . . . I always knew you were a Jew-lover . . . a nigger lover . . ."

After the first couple of threatening phone calls, I let the answering machine pick up the rest. It was a little intimidating to my mother. There were so many threats on my life and even my mother's that she finally turned the tapes over to the police for evidence. Death threats didn't intimidate me, because I already knew they were coming. The rabbis and Rick, however, were quite concerned about the whole thing. After all, they had asked me to join forces with the Simon Wiesenthal Center in the first place.

Shortly after I began speaking out against intolerance, against my old lifestyle, against hatred, I went to court in Victorville, California, in relation to my boys' custody. I missed them so badly. One of the biggest problems I faced was that there was no past case history where racist behavior alone had cost a mother her children. My lawyer told reporters, "We know that Nicole will raise those children as white supremacists, which is not in their best interest."

At the trial, Nicole continued to deny having any knowledge of the Skinhead Movement or of white supremacy. Evidence—including photos and videotapes of her in 1989 doing the Nazi salute at the front of a fire at a swastika burning and also in 1993 at a white power baby shower—wasn't enough. A court-appointed psychologist interviewed both Nicole and I.

He had concerns about her "past ties" to neo-Nazi groups, but he also had concerns about my past and much uncertainty about my break-off with the Movement. Apparently, it hadn't been long enough to establish a track record. His recommendation was that the court grant continued custody to my ex-wife, even though Nicole never publicly renounced the Movement. I was sick inside.

The judge took his recommendation but also demanded that Nicole had to bring the kids back to California in two weeks. Two weeks later, Nicole appeared in court, but she didn't bring the kids. I was missing them terribly. I was so used to being with them that all I had felt since they were gone was a horrible emptiness inside of me. I couldn't believe she wouldn't bring my Tommy and Konrad back to court, at least so I could see them, hug them, and let them know how much I loved them.

"I brought them to California," said Nicole to the judge, "but I'm not bringing them to court." The judge was not happy with her.

"I want to live in Washington," she continued, and went on to tell the judge that she was a shift manager at McDonald's. However, the judge ruled that she had to move back to California or the kids would go into my custody. She was ordered to stay within a hundred mile radius of me, and within the state of California. Angry that she was being forced back to California, two weeks later Nicole moved in with her brother in Santa Monica, one hundred miles from me, as far away as she could get. I didn't care. I was overjoyed to see my kids and to know that they were safe. At least I would be able to influence their lives for good in short periods. I had to keep thinking positive thoughts or go crazy about the whole thing. At least they would have the chance to know how much I loved them. It was heart-wrenching, but the court did schedule another hearing where I thought I might be able to prevail.

Our divorce was made final in court on December 5 of that year, the same day of my first appearance on *48 Hours*. In the court proceedings they asked if I wanted a divorce. I answered affirmatively. They asked Nicole, and she wouldn't answer the judge. The judge said, "The client needs to answer the question—yes or no." Nicole started crying. She finally said yes, and the judge proclaimed us legally divorced. She didn't seem too happy, for what reason I have no clue. She had told me many times that she didn't love me. After that she became my worst nightmare. Death threats were nothing compared to this.

"Are you sure you want to continue with this?" the rabbis asked me.

They were afraid something might go beyond threatening my life. They were afraid someone from a local or national organization would try to make good on the threats. I had some situations that came up from my sudden appearances on TV. A few old "friends" stopped by my place. One old gang member called and had the guts to ask me to go to coffee with him.

"Sure!" I said. "You bring a friend, and I'll bring some friends."

"Oh, no, TJ," he said, his voice wheedling. "I want to see you. I want to talk to you about what's going on. Let's just you and me meet." Well, as the old adage goes, I may be dumb, but I'm not stupid—unlike the idiots that accidentally blew up my mailbox in the middle of the night when they didn't shut it correctly and the wind blew it open, tripping the bomb mechanism they had placed there.

A few weeks later, Tom Metzger even posted the local bar I hung out at on his website. Some FBI friends tipped me off to that as well. Yeah, they were definitely looking for an opportunity. On *48 Hours*, Tom admitted, "He's put himself in a bad situation." When the journalist asked if I was in danger, Metzger replied, "I don't know, but I think that he'll probably spend many years looking over his shoulder. It annoys me that a white man would totally turn to join this gang at the Simon Wiesenthal Center," added Tom. "These people that would destroy our Bill of Rights if they get a chance. Anyone who would join a group that would want to cut my freedom of speech off is a deadly enemy." Then Tom started claiming he had never met me and that I was never at his home.

It didn't help that the Wiesenthal Center was in the spotlight of the Movement all the time. The center's pledge to work toward tolerance and world peace as well as the rabbis' influence with world leaders made the center a menace to the white power way of life. My teaming up with them made them a bigger threat in the Movement's eyes. A white power Skins' website portrays the racists' point of view about the Wiesenthal Center: "Rabbi Abraham Cooper of the Museum of Tolerance, a veritable 'house of pain' in Los Angeles, where one can pay to be indoctrinated in the Jewish opinion of what hate is all about. As usual, it centers on their own perpetual victim status. Why Mr. Cooper was interviewed is uncertain, although the media always goes to a Jewish 'expert' when considering any discussion of white power. Perhaps it was because he ran the museum's spy network that tracks all of the white power groups across the country."

There are other sites that claimed Rabbi Cooper is a secret Massad agent, which illustrated their fear. Racists and separatists felt threatened however, because the center, like the Anti-Defamation League (ADL) and the Southern Poverty Law Center (SPLC) strictly monitor the Movement. While Rabbi Hier and Rabbi Cooper were used to the pressure of hate groups, they were extremely worried about me. I educated them on the fact that for nearly fifteen years, everybody in the world had hated me except my gang buddies and a few members of my family that refused to give up on me. When I had been a Skin, I had developed the attitude of not caring what other people thought. This time I was determined to use that attitude toward something positive—something that would make a difference in the world.

Like Rabbi Cooper, I took it as a badge of honor when a Marty Cox or a Tom Metzger called me a race traitor. During interviews for the History Channel for the *Gangland* series, Tom and Marty both suggested that I was the biggest threat to the Movement. Obviously I was doing so much damage that leaders tried to belittle me to solidify their own standing. Dr. William Pierce called me a closet homosexual while others have said I was a U.S. military plant or an FBI plant, used to infiltrate the Skinhead Movement. I laughed at that one, wondering when the FBI started recruiting fifteen-year-olds. Kenneth Alfred Strom was another white supremacy preacher who used to bad-mouth me, but he was convicted of child pornography. When racists call me a Jew-lover or a nigger-lover, I know it's because I've awakened to the beauty that lies in each one of us—and that is the biggest threat to hate.

I started to see the difference I was making with my speaking within just a few months, which was satisfying. I started counting the kids that I knew I had pulled away from gangs, only counting the kids I knew for sure. For example, one girl came up to me in Bakersfield a year after I started. "Do you remember me from last year when you came to speak to our group?" she asked. I nodded. She was easy to remember. "Well, I want you to know you changed my life," she said. "I'm in with a group of kids that went on to college. That's where I am now." I was very pleased and smiled widely at her and congratulated her. Before I could get a big head about it, however, she added, "I figured if a dumb-ass like you could turn your life around, well, surely I could." That was one comment I will never forget. It continues to keep me humble.

Once when I was in Riverside giving a presentation to youngsters, an old nemesis, Dale Jensen from the San Bernardino's Sheriff Department, was there as well. He had heard I was speaking out against the Movement and he came—very skeptically—to see if I was for real. Several of the officers I had once been in negative contact with in my Skinhead days also came. Some of them believed that I had really changed and turned my back forever. Some of them believed that I never could (after all, they thought, they knew me in the day, and in addition, a firm belief runs rampant among officers: "Once a Skinhead, always a Skinhead." They have a right to believe that, and 99 percent of the time, that has proven itself to be true.) Some in this group of officers believed that what I was doing with the center was all for show.

After the presentation, Dale Jensen came up and I could tell he really wanted to talk to me. He wanted to see if what I presented was reality. We talked for a long time that afternoon. He told my writer later that he left that presentation only "skeptically going to give me a chance." He needed to see evidence of change. I have to give the guy credit. He kept in touch with me and watched everything I did, everything I said, including evidence I gave police to find the bad guys. He particularly watched for consistency. Dale finally witnessed that once I turned my back on the Movement, I had sincerely committed myself to making a real difference—to be an actual contribution to society rather than the detriment I had been for so many years.

"This is an individual who was extremely committed to the Movement," Dale said, "and who saw where the Movement was going and made a point to leave it. Anybody can get up and talk about where they are going and where they've been. In TJ's case, not only was he involved in it and believed it, but when it turned out *not* to be what he thought it was, he left, despite the negative consequences. He reached a point where he was deemed extremely loyal. Not only to leave the Movement, but then also to denounce it was a big thing. TJ was the first guy with enough guts to do it. There's no denying that he had connections. It's no lie that there was a desire for others in the Movement to send him a clear, deliberate message for leaving. As a matter of fact, there are still people who think it is their duty and responsibility to make sure he's dead—he knows too much and needs to go."

Despite the threats, life became so interesting to me. For a long time I negated what I had to contribute. Then I realized that this Movement had touched a lot of kids around the nation. It has been in the States for three decades. Before most of today's white power leaders had been

Klansmen, Nazis, or National Alliance members, they were Skinheads first. Eric Glibe, who runs the National Alliance, was once a Skinhead. Also, Matt Hales, a leader for the World Church of the Creator, was also one. In the Klan and other groups, Skinheads are the reason these groups are even still alive today.

In the late seventies white power was marginalized and almost dead. Then the Skinhead Movement came along, which was nothing that they had created. It was a subculture that split into two factions. White supremacist saw the opportunity and began to take advantage of it.

NEW COMRADES, BETTER COMPANY

It was valuable to me to know what their ideologies and philosophies were, what they wanted to accomplish, and through what means they hoped to gain power. I had been able to assist many people to see different perspectives and to know what to watch for, whether it was with their own children, or with bosses, doctors, lawyers, and professors—anyone they might come into contact with.

I never knew what amazing new people I would meet and what old associates I might come into contact with. We were invited to Gonzoga State University in Washington State to speak at a conference on a panel discussing anti-Semitism and racism with Mark Weitzman. I was honored to be in the room with this highly intelligent person who brought a wealth of knowledge of the world in general, from politics to the racist movement—especially the intellectual side to the racist philosophy. He could easily take on Dr. Pierce, Pastor Butler, or any other Holocaust denier. When I arrived, Michael Hoffman, racist and author, was protesting the conference and *me. Wow!* I thought. *Look at this ripple.* He had signs out there that said "TJ Leyden is a liar" and "Simon Wiesenthal was a liar." I wondered if he wanted to take his book back that he had autographed for me years earlier, when he had written, "To TJ: Best wishes in this great battle. Michael A. Hoffman." The university officials were going to ask him to leave. They were on the radio to the security guards to escort him off campus.

"Heck, let him protest," I said, chuckling alongside of Mark. "Let him have his freedom of speech. Let people see who Michael Hoffman really is." We had close to three hundred people in the auditorium listening to our conference. Michael had one other guy helping him with signs, and no one was really listening. Sometime during the conference,

Hoffman's protests attracted some media coverage for himself, and then actually back-lashed because it gave us much more media coverage. By the time I came out, he was gone.

I couldn't care less that Michael Hoffman called me a liar. In a world where kids have become more afraid of gang members than they are of the police, I knew it was time to make a difference, that it was time to do some real work in education. At that moment I realized that I was in the best of company . . . and that I would continue to be in the best of company for the rest of my life.

19

REDEMPTION—
FROM HATE TO HOPE

WORKING AT THE Wiesenthal Center quickly became a way of life for me. I found that I actually became a great asset to their group and the message they were sending to the world for peace and tolerance. As often as three times a day, six days a week, I spoke to audiences about who I was, where I came from, and what I'd learned about tolerance versus hate. At the center, there were always those visitors who didn't believe me or my message. At first, I took it so personally, and I went out of my way to make those people believe me. Later I realized it was my responsibility to disseminate information, and whether they took it or not was their choice.

For the first month and a half that I spoke at the Wiesenthal Center, I didn't get paid. Avra, the head of public relations for the center, the museum, and Mariah Films, felt that it couldn't continue that way. She told me she appreciated my passion and commitment, and at some point she went to the rabbis.

"We can't keep having TJ come here every day and not get paid. He comes eighty-seven miles each way, every day!" The rabbis agreed, and they gave me some money for travel. A few weeks later, however, Rabbi Cooper asked me if I would consider speaking full time. I told him I would, but that I would have to quit my job. I took a huge cut in pay—making only half of what I was making before. I did my best not to get nervous about it. I had a custody battle and wanted to be the best dad I could be for my sons, but money was no longer a driving force in what I did. For me, my new work became a way to pay back society. In addition, the possibility of being able to use my gifts, talents, and tools in a positive way was the catalyst for not only a big change in me, but a chance to make a huge difference in the world. I also knew that the rabbis would not have offered this full-time position to me if they hadn't believed in me. I was very honored by their trust.

FAMILY DYNAMICS

Living one hundred miles away from the boys was really tough. I had moved into a nice apartment complex, and Nicole was having problems with her roommate who was stealing from her and causing her financial difficulties. The apartment next to me was open, so I paid for her first and last month's rent, and my mom helped her find a job. I was so glad to see my kids, though she wouldn't often let me have them. At least I could glimpse them in their everyday lives and they knew I was there for them. Since I was traveling to my speaking engagements, Nicole took me to court for teaching tolerance too much. All I was asking for was for every other Thursday night and Friday to be with the boys.

"It is really important to me that I have time and opportunity to be with my children," I explained to the judge, trying not to get emotional. I couldn't bear to think of having them ripped away from me again. "I am busy with work, but I make time to see them—I *have* to be able to see them."

"Do you have the ability to take care of your children?" the judge asked.

I explained my solid work situation and my flexible schedule.

"In addition, Nicole lives in apartment No. 4, and I live in No. 5 in the same complex. I would like to see the boys as much as possible, and so I made sure they could be still close to their mother if they need her."

"That's weird," the judge said, a bit perplexed. "Okay, I will grant you week-to-week custody.

"No, no!" cried Nicole. "I'll give him every other Thursday!"

"No," the judge said firmly, "I ruled that custody is to go week-to-week."

I was so glad to get the boys more often and be able to spend the time with them that we wanted. It was such a great thing for our relationship and for me to be an actual, important part of their lives. They were a priceless part of mine.

MAKING THE MESSAGE MOST IMPORTANT

At the center, there were some political issues that were a little tough for me. In a strange way, some of the people who worked there had issues with the fact that I was suddenly waltzed in and now had the privilege of attending dinners and VIP meetings with the rabbis. I couldn't blame them and realized I might have felt the same way in their shoes. The rabbis wanted people to meet me because of the major change I had made. Many people were shocked by it, but it attracted a lot of interest and brought heightened awareness of current hate groups, their philosophies, and what they were capable of doing to our nation and our world. Others at the center were incredibly welcoming, like Rick and Avra. I also appreciated Jamie, who did all the graphic design and multi-media for the initial book that I helped to get published through the Simon Wiesenthal Center—*The Lexicon of Hate*. After I developed the concept, she helped me to bring it to fruition. It has served many organizations in the fight against hatred and violence.

During every speech, I always spoke with the desire that some kids and adults would be inspired to turn their lives around. From August until December of 1996, I made over 100 appearances. In 1997, I made over 300, and over the next five years I would speak to over 1,800 groups of people. I remembered in my past when I had influenced huge groups of people. My intent before was to gain power and control. Now I didn't care what people thought about me. I cared what they were learning about the world and the message I was bringing.

Some appearances were short and simple. I often spoke at the Hate Map in the Museum of Tolerance to groups of people such as school children and tour groups. As they came to learn more, I would give part of a lecture for fifteen or twenty minutes. Other appearances were actual interviews or full lectures at universities, to law enforcement groups, and to different branches of the military.

In the beginning I worked my guts out. I kept seeing the faces of some of the kids I had brought into the Movement, and they would haunt me. I wanted to do whatever I could to make up for that. However, I didn't know that I was literally burning myself out. I flew to New York three to five times a year to spend a week at the center's affiliate office there. They also had one in Miami and one in Canada. I would travel to these locations as well and speak to as many groups as the center could schedule in a week's time.

Trips to New York were very interesting for me and a little different. People often went by what I dressed like as opposed to my message. Some would make the craziest comments on my appearance and think that I was not as believable as if I were wearing a three-piece suit. I often wore cowboy boots (I *am* from the West) and sometimes jeans and T-shirts. Once I wore a hat representing the Arizona Diamondbacks, one of my favorite teams. One person thought the initial *A* stood for Aryan. He didn't believe me when I told him it represented the team. Obviously I didn't wear that hat again during a speech.

Whether in LA or New York or Miami, I would go to law enforcement agencies, talk to educators, and do fundraising events or free events for people who were major contributors to the center. I was glad to have Rick or Avra with me at each of these speeches. Rick was a mentor and a friend, and Avra was my confidant. I found out much later that Rick was also Jewish.

"How can you be Jewish?" I asked incredulously. "You're eating a cheeseburger! This morning you had bacon and eggs!"

Rick laughed. "Not all Jews do the diet," he explained. He taught me a lot about Jewish sects, and it reminded me a lot of Christianity's various churches and differing beliefs. I had never known there was so much diversity within the Jewish culture. At one of my speaking engagements in Canada, I met another Jew that continued to open my perspectives. His name was David Lazzar, and he was a youth counselor at a Jewish conference for teens. He was a brilliant musician who taught Jewish children about the roots of their beliefs through music. That didn't sound like such a shocker to me until I learned that his band and others that he promoted were heavy metal. They incorporated their teachings with the sound that teens like. In other words, David did for Jewish teens what Stryper did for Christians in the eighties.

David's band and their music used lyrics that taught kids about their Jewish ancestry, beliefs, values, and scriptures, and his lyrics were positive, creative, and uplifting. As excited as I was (and, yes, a little surprised) to find a Jew using heavy metal as a tool, I asked David his story. He had once been a metal head and into drugs. When he found God, it turned his life around. His was another transformational story. We became fast friends.

I made a lot of other interesting friends over the years, including two police officers that I came to deeply respect for what they did for our communities. Of course they were very doubtful of me to begin with, and I didn't blame them. Over the years, we came to have a mutual understanding and respect.

A beautiful thing began to happen within my psyche the longer I worked at the center. For example, I always knew that the Holocaust really had taken place (there was far too much evidence to the contrary), but when I was in the Movement I was good at pushing the whole thing as a lie. As a spin-monster, I had been excellent at denying it and getting others to deny it, just as I had been in saying that slavery wasn't bad. For so many years I had said, "Hey, we educated blacks. We doubled their life span." At the center, I came face to face with many of the people, the stories, and the situations that were caused from this type of disjointed thinking. I met Holocaust survivors and heard their stories. Elizabeth Mann was the first Holocaust survivor I ever met.

Avra and Michelle set me up to come to lunch with them and Elizabeth. This woman had been a survivor as a young woman and she told me the story of when her family arrived at Auschwitz. Some of the details have been burned into her memory, and as she described the story to me, I felt like I was there, seeing what she saw, and feeling exactly what she had felt.

When they stepped off the train at Auschwitz, her family members were forced to separate at gunpoint. They took the men off to one side, young women on the other, while mothers with younger children stayed in the middle. Elizabeth's brother had just celebrated his bar mitzvah. In Jewish culture, that would have made him a young man, and he would have gone with his father. During the train ride, however, he had gotten terribly sick. Elizabeth was worried about him. She took him aside and told him to go with his mother, thinking that he would be safer and watched over through his illness. With tears streaming down her cheeks, Elizabeth described finding out that all of the women and children from that train were sent straight into the gas chamber. Her tears became my own as I felt the wrenching pain of a young girl who found she had sent her brother to his death, when she thought she was saving his life.

That was a very emotional experience for me. We became fast friends as I worked at the Wiesenthal Center, and whenever I would see her, I would give her a hug. I read other articles and books and heard lectures about slavery and hate crimes, things people had endured on the other side of hatred and bigotry. So not only did I turn my back on the Movement, I also turned to face and embrace those that I had shunned and ignorantly committed acts of violence against for so many years.

Day to day, being around a multitude of people at the center was eye-opening. From the people who worked there to those who visited from around the world, I got to know Jews, homosexuals, as well as many bi-racial and multi-ethnic people from hundreds of different cultures—and all in an environment of promoting cultural and religious understanding. It was such a stark contrast from the masculine, misogynistic way of life I'd lived, and it was fascinating to me.

In doing presentations all over the United States and Canada, I met lots of Jewish leaders and other religious leaders from many faiths as well and began to have great respect for them. Another dynamic Jew became actively involved in my life change. Dr. Karl Stein, with the help of the Grossman Burn Center, donated his time and resources to the painstak-ing (and extremely painful) goal of the removal of my twenty-nine tattoos over a three-year span. Unfortunately it was found that he could only take care of some of them. I contracted skin cancer as a result of the treatments and had to stop. We discovered that I have a rare form of skin immunity. The laser destroyed the natural melatonin in the skin pigment and caused me to be highly susceptible to melanoma. I'm grateful to Dr. Stein for the ones he could remove, however. We worked on my neck first, then my arms and hands, removing only three. While I would have given anything to have the rest taken off, I was glad the old, hate-filled tattoos could be covered up with more positive images, and I ended up still having twenty-six reworked tattoos.

When people saw my tattoos—despite my removal and makeover efforts—they had automatic assumptions about who I was and what I stood for. One night I came back from a long week of speaking engage-ments, and I was bone-tired. I was driving home from the airport around midnight in my car with tinted windows. A suspicious cop pulled me over. He saw all my tattoos and I know he was thinking, *I've really got someone here!* I wasn't going to argue with him. I hadn't done anything wrong, so I sat on the curb calmly as he searched my car for weapons, drugs, or anything else he thought he could pin on me. Another officer pulled up behind him as backup. This one happened to be an officer I was familiar with from the San Bernardino Sheriff's Department. He not only knew me, but also knew of my mission.

"What are you doing sitting on the curb, TJ?" he asked incredulously. He looked at the other officer. "Don't you know who this is?" The other officer shook his head. "This is TJ Leyden. Yeah, he looks like a bad-ass because he used to be a Hammerskin, but he works at the Simon Wiesenthal Center and now he trains officers and military about the Movement. I've seen some of his trainings. He's pretty good." The first officer couldn't believe it.

"Why the hell didn't you just tell me who you were?" he asked a bit sheepishly.

"Would you have believed me?" I asked him. He stared at all my tattoos and shook his head with an emphatic *no*.

Through these and other experiences, I began learning the art of stepping out of judgment of people myself, especially assumptions based on appearances. I knew for a fact that many of my former associates who were now in powerful positions in the Movement looked like nice, upstanding community citizens and businessmen in suits and ties. Fat chance. Their primary motivation was to blow the country to hell and rebuild it to their specifications. They were just waiting for the chance.

I also learned quickly that there were a lot of really good people trying to make the world a better place, even if they dressed like the dregs of society. The first few times I went to law enforcement conferences to speak, several of the undercover police agents scared the pants off of me. Later when they came up to talk to me when I finished speaking, it allowed me the opportunity to get to know them. All of these experiences added to looking at people in a truer depth than their appearance, skin color, race, religion, or whatever. When I found myself stepping into judgment of anyone, that's when I began to realize that they were probably someone that I could learn a great deal from. I also tried to help people that judged me the most harshly.

One group that I came to really enjoy teaching was military: officers and personnel. I liked enlightening them about situations within their own processes that they didn't know. On several occasions I was asked to do deep level trainings so that situations such as the DC Sniper could be prevented in the future and not come back to bite them in the butt. I taught them how to be diligently looking for the warning signs of a person like the sniper, even if he seems like a passive racist. One of the main principles I tried to drill into them was that anytime they found a passive racist, they should stop training him. A great illustration of this was Timothy McVeigh. The military should have stopped training him when he was passing out copies of *The Turner Diaries*. They should have kicked him out. They should have stopped training me as well. It needs to be an ongoing safety policy in the military. Our military has been famous for training some far right-wing racists with deep-seated ideologies of hate. In the past when these racists were caught, their hands were simply slapped and they have been sent on their way. Punishment has been next to nothing, sending a clear signal that the Movement could continue to send men to get the best military training on the face of the earth, and by doing so, further their malevolent cause.

For example, in 2001 in Norfolk, Virginia, a group of five sailors were arrested for trying to make a hydrogen bomb. They were only three components shy of creating an explosive devise that could have wiped out much of the entire East coast. Three of them were card-carrying members of the Movement. The remaining two owned more racist paraphernalia than the other three combined . . . and yet all five were allowed to finish their tours. Sure, they received a reduction in ranks, cut allowances, and were "not allowed to have anything more to do with the nuclear area" in their work. *Really?* (Sarcasm intended.) I have wanted to scream, *Is that all? WHY?* This is not a couple of kids working experiments in someone's basement. These were card-carrying separatists with the desire to overthrow the government. Armed with this knowledge, I set to work to wake up the U.S. Military.

Another prime example took place at Fort Lewis in Washington State, where an Army Ranger had "Aryan Warrior" tattooed on his back. The Army didn't do anything about it, even though this ranger was a top man in EOD—Explosive Ordinances and Demolitions. In addition, the FBI had taken his picture at a rally at Richard Butler's compound in Idaho. The Army knew of his racist affiliations and that he was someone the military had fully trained to blow things up—and do it extremely well, by the way—but politically they felt their hands were tied. Apparently, someone has to take the fall if a person is kicked out of the military and decides to sue. Luckily, some guys from Fort Lewis heard my speech at Fort Bragg and when they went back they said, "At least stop *training* the guy!" Luckily, this advice was taken, and the ranger was not allowed to re-enlist.

RECLAIMING OLD TERRITORY
IN A POSITIVE WAY

Believe it or not, another favorite audience of mine was my old ene-mies in law enforcement. I came to have tremendous respect for these guys. I saw how hard they worked to keep guys like I used to be off the streets and make them safe for the rest of the world to go on living. One of the major problems I have witnessed within gang units has been the high turnover of new officers. So many officers go in and out of the units that the gang cops haven't always known dangerous people who used to be on the radar even a few months before. Just because someone wasn't on the radar for a year doesn't mean they're not dangerous. My sabbatical in the Marines was a good case in point. I did far more damage in fostering hatred and recruiting *after* I went into the Marines than before I went in. Though I may have become smarter and less publicly violent, I was more dangerous as the enforcer that no one suspected. Then, when I got out of the Marines, I found out that all of my previous information had been wiped clean off most of the police databases! The poor guys had to start from scratch on rebuilding information on me, and they had to do it fast. After joining the Wiesenthal Center, I began to teach law enforcement how to keep backup files of information on criminals and look at easier ways of cross-referencing information between counties and emphasized the need for this as well as between states and even nations. Case in point: Hammerskins are an international group, and one of the largest gangs in the entire world.

I came to realize that the police did the best they could with the knowledge they had. Therefore it was my honor and privilege to give them more knowledge and training to help them in the fight against violence. When they would see so much garbage happening on the streets, it was easy for them to become disillusioned with what they did and therefore extremely suspicious of me at first. Some of them even believed that I hadn't really changed, that I was a spy, or that I was only doing this for the money. I didn't fight with them when I realized they have to fight enough already. I changed my focus to educate, educate, educate.

I'll never forget the cop that came up to me and said, "I hope your children turn out just the way you *were*." I've tried to forget about him and remember the cop whose son got mixed up with Skins and ended up going to prison for a long time. I try to remember the pain he was in when he came to talk to me—and how he had wished he had known some of the things I was teaching before I had finally been invited to speak to his department. I try to remember those that I really *can* help, when I can get my message out, and when they take it as it is meant—to help them in their everyday lives as police officers, parents, and community leaders.

My all-time favorite audience was the middle and high school kids. As a goal-driven person, I made it a point to try to get at least eighty youth out of the Movement, for the eighty kids I personally had brought in. I knew I had influenced and indoctrinated many, many more than that toward hate, and I felt gut-wrenching aches—intensely physical pain at times when I would think of the kids I had brought in, and what had happened to many of them. I continued to have nightmares that included these kids or faces of the victims that I had hurt in the past. I hadn't let any of this bother me before, but now I had begun to look at life very, very differently—thinking so differently, feeling so differently than I ever had. In speaking out, my spirit was trying to tell the world that I had made a mistake, but that I had changed. Still, deep down I felt that I could never make up for the places some of these kids had taken their lives, because of the role I had played in it when I was a Skin.

Kids are so smart, and they captured my new message quickly—perhaps more quickly than they want to sometimes. I have talked to more than one group of youngsters, little wannabe bangers who were wearing their pants around their ankles, showing off their boxer shorts—supposedly such a hot look. Well, they were hotter than they could even guess.

"Do you know where that style you are sporting comes from?" I asked a group of kids. They all cheered.

"Yeah, from prison, man—prison gangs," said one. "It's so cool!" said another.

"That's right," I told them, nodding. "Some guys in prison gangs sport this look. Those are the guys that have to use their ASS-ets to survive in prison. We call them *punks*." It took a minute, but then suddenly I saw all these guys pulling up their pants nice and high . . .

It became clear to me that kids need education. They do things because of what they see on TV, in the movies, at home, and on the streets. Just like me when I was their age, our society's children just want to fit in, they want to belong. This means having a safe place to call home and someone to watch their back. Unless they know better—from school, or parents, or church or their community—they'll do whatever it takes, including joining a gang to get what they need. The movie *Colors* brought a sharp rise in recruits and gang activity and violence all around the nation. So did Geraldo Rivera's talk show portraying the Skinheads in a much too powerful light. Kids are prone to following the crowd and to identifying themselves with the latest fads. That's where I hoped to step in, to provide an alternate point of view and a paradigm shift in critical thinking.

When MTV approached the Simon Wiesenthal Center about doing a Public Service Announcement on MTV, I was all for it, because I couldn't think of a better way than a music channel to capture young kids' attention. The commercial series was called "Fight for Your Rights—Take a Stand Against Violence." Judy Shepherd aired in a commercial about hate crimes against homosexuals. Mine was against racism. I know some kids paid attention because for several months after the campaign, they still made comments about it when I came out to visit their schools or groups. I would like to see more campaigns, more commercials like that one that actually reaches kids.

When I went to speak at a place like a school or community center, and I saw a kid's face change from the time I got in there until the time I left, I knew I had made an impression. I would hope that impression was enough to make him question what he hears and sees on the street and in the media, and even in his family, if it's detrimental. Kids need that alternate point of view about tolerance, about seeing the other side, and about peace.

I also enjoyed speaking to and teaching college kids. Their minds would absorb so much as they were figuring out how they want to contribute to the world when they graduate. I was asked to speak at many colleges around the United States, and I loved it when I would receive emails from students and professors, as many as twenty at a time, asking for more information. That was unbelievably exciting to me, because it meant that people were learning to think critically about what was taking place on the streets across the country. I knew from experience that when people were active learners, they were much less likely to be complacent bystanders. It was exciting to me to inspire people to take positive action.

Working at the center became my life. I continued to travel back and forth 174 miles a day, every day, unless I was traveling to talks three times a week. As intriguing as all this was, I was getting burned out. I started drinking a lot when I was home as a self-medicating technique. I still hadn't gotten over all my inner battles and the inner demons that haunted me. For one thing, I was incredibly lonely. My family was my only support, except for a few people at the Wiesenthal Center. Every good friend I ever had was gone, and half of those people wanted a bullet in me. I also had to be extremely careful where I went. I couldn't go to any of the places I used to hang out at: no gun shows, and definitely no bars in Huntington Beach, Costa Mesa, Anaheim Hills, Redlands, or Yucaipa. While I was used to watching my back all the time from enemies, now I had to watch my back from old friends who knew me—knew my habits, my likes and dislikes, my hobbies, and so forth. I had multiple enemies all over the place, and I knew a lot of people on all sides now. Inwardly, too, I was still fighting a lot of my own racism. I would notice that certain things would set me off, like local, national, and international events. Sometimes it was just as simple as someone looking at me funny. I had to fight the anger that still lingered so near the surface—it frightened me because there were times I would want to act out the warring instinct I had honed for so many years.

One night I got a DUI and was sentenced to alcohol school. I didn't have enough time with my schedule to make the school, so a year later when it wasn't complete the judge sent me to jail for a month. There I had to be quarantined—isolated under protective custody because of my many enemies in the Movement and my new affiliation with the Wiesenthal Center. Serving time sucked, but it gave me a lot to think about. My life was coming apart, and I needed to do something about it—I just didn't know what.

The rabbis started noticing things coming apart too, and they got me a therapist. This was one of the best, most miraculous things that ever happened to me. I was able for the first time to be open and honest about my childhood, anger issues, frustration, and inner rage. I went to therapy for four and a half years with Dr. Aaron Hass. He helped me to understand so many things, and how much of my anger stemmed from my parents' divorce, the emotional abuse I endured as a little kid, and then carrying it into adulthood, never having dealt with it. I even got to express feelings to my parents about my childhood. That was hard and yet so healing.

These miracles never would have happened if it wasn't for the rabbis believing in me, supporting me, and helping me. They gave me a chance to redeem myself. I will always remember them and respect them. I even grew to love them deeply.

In particular, I watched Rabbi Cooper closely. I decided that if I could have half the impact on the world that he has had, that would be amazing. I watched him with his daughters and witnessed what a good father and mentor he was. Whenever I was an idiot or screwing up, he would help me to face it, but at the same time, he would say, "How do we get around this—how do we fix this?" He walked alongside me on one of the most difficult paths I've ever taken, and I became incredibly grateful for the gifts that he, Rabbi Hier, Rick, and the other staff at the Wiesenthal Center were to me.

20

SECOND CHANCES

IT AMAZED ME to find what kinds of opportunities could happen in life when I was focused on great things: great experiences, great expectations, and great people. Once I started on this path, things fell into place more easily than they ever had. I still had my challenges; some of my old habits died HARD. I had to start over with new, positive friends, situations, and people. It didn't happen all at once, but as it developed, I knew I was being watched over. My mother knew it too. And she kept praying for me.

One night, shortly after I'd done the commercial for MTV in the late nineties, I was out at the Cocky Bull, country dancing with some new friends of mine and delighted that some beautiful women were there as well. One gorgeous woman, Julie Jalayne Camp, was talking to some people we both knew. I had decided to quit drinking for a while, and I liked how it felt. Julie noticed we were both drinking non-alcoholic beers, and we started talking. We actually talked a lot that night, and I thought we really hit it off. I also thanked my lucky stars, because I was incredibly attracted to her.

Since I left the Movement, I found different ways to keep myself entertained at bars. Instead of getting drunk or fighting, I would get different girls to talk and dance with me. I'd always been a good talker, and it would irritate the hell out of my friends because I could get hot girls to keep me company. Julie was a girl that made them really jealous that night. She had gorgeous platinum blonde hair and an enticing figure. As we talked, though, I could tell that she was different, deeper. Not only was she fun, with a great sense of humor, but she was also incredibly intelligent and engaging to talk with.

I went home knowing I really liked this girl and I wanted to see her again. Unfortunately, I had grown up playing games with women—especially the ones that I liked. I played a game of hard-to-get that dealt a vicious blow.

The next weekend, I went to that same bar, hoping that Julie would be there. Unfortunately I had a date that was set from two weeks prior. Julie *did* come to the bar, hoping I'd be there. When she saw me with my date, she didn't want anything to do with me and I didn't really get a chance to explain. A friend of mine ended up taking her and her girlfriend to another bar, and I ended up getting kicked out of the first one for trying to get my underage friend in. She would have been twenty-one in about ten days from then, and I didn't see the harm at the time. Like I said, some habits were still dying hard, even as other parts of my life were falling into place.

My friend asked her to the rodeo the next weekend and I saw her there. Like an idiot, I started drinking to make it easier to talk to her. I got a little bit lit up, and I tried to kiss her in the parking lot by the trucks.

"What are you doing?" she cried, backing away from me. She couldn't believe I was trying to kiss her when she was there with another person.

"I like you," I said lamely.

"Well, it's too late!" she said. End of story, at least for a while.

Julie dated my friend for a year and a half and, in the interim, introduced me to one of her friends. We were close for a while then broke up, while Julie and I remained friends. We could just talk to each other and relate on so many levels. I didn't want to interfere with her relationship, but I didn't want to lose her as a friend, either. I always had a secret hope . . .

On February 4, 2001, I went to the bar, knowing she was coming and that her relationship, with her boyfriend was very rocky. I had a sharp longing to see her. Deep within both of us, there was a mutual attraction, growing friendship and genuine respect. She wasn't being treated very well in her current relationship, and I knew if she were to ever date me, I would treat her like a queen. It turned out that she was ready for someone who would give her the courtesy, kindness, and abiding love that she deserved. After almost two years of solid friendship, she knew she could trust me. Instantaneously, we became serious about each other.

In the beginning, I was worried that Julie might freak out about my past. She knew I spoke about tolerance and hate groups, but there was no delicate way for her to know how involved I had once been in the Movement. She knew I had worked at the Museum of Tolerance for many years now, but she didn't know much more than that. As soon as we got together, however, she started doing many of my bookings for speaking engagements and going to the Museum of Tolerance with me. In short order she found out everything else about me, and loved me anyway. That was the second miracle in my life.

"What do you love about her?" a friend of mine asked, when I was so delighted to be with her, I didn't want any other woman.

"Everything!" I said. "Absolutely everything. Julie is the most incredible thing in my life."

On a day toward the end of March, Julie was sitting next to me as I was driving down the freeway toward the museum. She popped a somewhat unexpected question.

"Have you ever thought about marrying me?" she asked, fishing around. *Two could play that game*, I thought.

"Sure, I'll marry you," I said. "Thanks for asking!"

She was a little flummoxed. "I didn't ask you!"

"Hey, that sounds like a proposal to me." She just grinned. We knew it was what we both wanted.

We planned the wedding for October, but soon we bumped the date up—way up! Personally, I had waited almost two years to be with the woman I loved, and I couldn't bear to wait any longer. We were married May 19, 2001.

After we married, Julie and I wanted her to quit the airlines and work full-time with me. I had talked with her about leaving Wiesenthal so I could be an expert witness in cases. I loved working at the center but had intense conflicts of interest that came up from time to time. Once I had evidence that could have freed a kid from false imprisonment. I wasn't allowed to testify. I passed the information onto someone else, and the kid never did jail time, thank goodness. But it was one of the hardest situations I'd ever gone through. I didn't want an innocent person to go to jail because of my restrictions. I passionately wanted the *real* bad guys in jail. I decided to go out on my own.

I developed a consulting firm called StrHATE Talk Consulting. With the assistance of CampusSpeak and other organizations, I was added to several speaker's bureaus and began doing talks around the country on my own. I also assisted law enforcement to really bringing down the bad guys. No longer restrained by a conflict of interest, I began to have several law enforcement agencies and others ask me to assist on specific cases. I helped with deciphering runes, taught the mentality of the Movement, and gave out a lot of inside information to help bring criminals down. It was very satisfying to me.

Julie quit her job at the airline and became a full-time mom. That meant no more traveling, which was delightful to me and her two boys and my two boys, who had grown to love her deeply as well. The most incredible thing to me was how well we fit together. We agreed on the most important things like moral values and ideals in our marriage and in rearing our children. In addition, I loved the fact that my mom and Julie have always gotten along so well. They had a lot in common. They both had the same problem—me.

From the beginning, Julie always inspired me to do more, to dig deeper, to grow taller. She even inspired me to quit drinking for good by laying down the law. On Halloween night of the year we were married, I was drinking and playing poker with my brother Mat.

"Looks like the pot is light a buck, TJ," he said and looked at me.

"What the hell are you talking about Mat, and why are you looking at me like that?"

"Because you took it," he said. I was infuriated. Why would I want to steal a stupid dollar? I socked him across the table—*hard*. That spurred one of the bloodiest fistfights I'd ever been involved in, even from my Skinhead days. Everyone in the room was screaming and freaking out, especially the two of us, grown "adult" and drunk men.

"I'm going to get my gun and shoot you," he said flatly. Other people stopped him, but that was enough for Julie. She'd had it. She also loved me enough to tell me the truth and to give me only one chance.

"If you EVER drink again," she swore, "I will leave you." I knew she meant it, and I was ashamed to have been involved in such a stupid altercation. I recognized the destructive part that alcohol had played in my life and was obviously still playing. I never had another drink. Nor have I ever desired it.

After I quit drinking, when Julie could tell I was sincere about being a good husband, father, and role model, we decided to have children of our own. We loved our four boys so much, and they were our pride and joy. We knew it would be awesome to create another child all our own between us as well.

Julie had been a member of The Church of Jesus Christ of Latter-day Saints all her life, although she had not been very active in the Church. Still, she had never, ever lost her testimony. When we became pregnant, Julie wanted our baby to be blessed in the LDS Church. I had studied enough religions and philosophies to know I didn't have any desire to get roped into anything. While I found different ideologies fascinating, even before my studies at the Wiesenthal Center, none of them had worked for me.

"Why don't you give me a Book of Mormon?" I asked. "So I can understand why this is so important to you. But don't get any ideas—I am not converting."

My mother-in-law gave me Julie's old copy of her scriptures right before I left for a two-day trip. By the time I returned, I had read all the way to Alma, in the middle of the thick book. I was intrigued, in spite of myself. I finally told her mother to have the missionaries stop by. I also told her not to get her hopes up. A couple of days later, two young men came by. I talked to them with such enthusiasm and passion in a way I don't think anyone ever talked to them during their entire two-year mission.

"I've got a bunch of questions," I told them. They answered as many as they could in the time we had, and I wanted more answers. I asked if they could come back the next day. They had other appointments, but agreed to return in a few days. By the time they visited three days later, I was done reading the Book of Mormon. They asked me to pray about it. But I already knew it was true, like nothing I'd ever read or known before in my life. At that point it was just formalities, but I still had more questions.

The missionaries came to teach me all the discussions so I would have a good background on The Church of Jesus Christ of Latter-Day Saints (Mormon) beliefs. My son, Tommy, asked to sit in on the discussions. He was eleven and was intrigued by the spirituality of these two young men and the changes he was beginning to witness in me in so short a time. We went through all the lessons.

Before the last lesson on baptism, the missionaries asked if I wanted to be baptized. Before I could answer, Tommy called out, "I want to be baptized!" Well, so did I, so we were baptized the same day: June 22, 2002. Shortly thereafter, my younger son, Konrad, started taking the lessons, as well. What we didn't know is that he had been listening in the hallway as Tommy and I were taking the lessons! When Konrad turned eight, I had the privilege of baptizing him—one of the greatest honors and blessings I had ever experienced.

Since then, I baptized and confirmed all my sons, except Gavyn, who was born later that year, and as of this writing is too young to be baptized. Mormons believe that the age of reason (being able to tell right from wrong) is the age of eight. Julie became active in the Church again too.

One thing that becoming a member of the LDS Church brought me was that I definitely became a better husband and father, and my kids have admitted that many times over. While some behaviors were more apparent than others, I became acutely aware of my responsibilities toward my sons, and how even little actions made a huge difference. Despite the incredible changes I made when turning away from the Movement, people who have known me best throughout the years say that I grew more since joining the Church than I ever did before.

There was one major ramification that I was not quite prepared for in my choice of religions. In all my years as a Skinhead, Nazi thug, and then as a traitor against the Movement, I never, EVER felt the sting of prejudice. People were afraid or suspicious of my tattoos, and some hated me for my actions, but I had never experienced the harsh, bitter side of blind bigotry, judgment, and discrimination until I became a member of the LDS Church. Surprisingly enough, people in this very conservative religion have embraced me and my family warmly and unconditionally. However, many people outside of my church have ridiculed me for my decision, told me I was crazy, wrong, stupid, ignorant, and even delusional for joining. When giving talks, I do not bring up my conversion to the general public. But when I'm answering questions, people have often said, "There has to be more to your change and how permanent and amazing it is. There must be something more." Well, of course, there has been, but as soon as they heard it—the fact that I became a Latter-day Saint—it disturbed some of them because it didn't fit within their own belief systems.

What these people didn't understand was the joy, love, and inspiration I found in my life in making this one, beautiful decision. Joining this church made a huge and dramatic impact on me. It seemed to take all I ever knew about God and pull it all together, and I became acutely aware of why I was here and a sense of God's plans for me. In addition, I learned as much from being the victim of this "reverse discrimination" as any experience I had been through. It absolutely served to make me a more compassionate person as well as a stronger member of my church. I learned what it is like on the other side of intolerance, and it's a lesson I will never forget.

21

THE HAND THAT ROCKS THE CRADLE

WHILE SOME PEOPLE have a sense of the philosophies of the White Power Movement, most don't understand the critical role that women play in it. Growing numbers of women are being attracted to the Movement for various reasons. Their impact on the Movement is substantially greater than most give them credit for.

Trends in advertising in the White Power Movement have changed to include a lot more women. Why? White separatists are not immune to the fact that sex sells—most particularly to their targeted audience of young, impressionable white males. Attractive Aryan women on the front cover and inside spreads draw in more males than guns and war. The truth is that women are a far more effective, magnetic pull to bring more men to the Movement than any other recruiting technique. In fact, women are currently the top targets for recruiters in the Movement, and women have even started to become recruiters too—and numbers are increasing.

Once indoctrinated to the cause, females teach their babies the philosophy about one world, one creed. The heart of the Movement begins at home. They teach their children that everyone else is the enemy, even subhuman. Therefore, they teach that all others don't deserve to live. Their desire is to raise an army of racist, bigoted killers. I know this first-hand, because at one time, Nicole and I had done the same.

On *Geraldo*, a young, racist Aryan woman admitted, "I think it's very brave to stand up for the race when it's socially unacceptable." She went on, "I want to be a desktop publisher and work at home and have a lot of babies with my husband. I want to put back into the white race what has been taken out of it."

People often think that men have to be the ones behind violent or militaristic movements. That is not always the case, as is increasingly shown in gang violence (regardless of race or gang affiliation) and also in the women of the White Power Movement. Girls don't have to be born into a gang to be hard-core racists, either. When someone in their family or a close friend buys into the propaganda, a woman will often follow and become equally or more dogmatic about those beliefs.

Lynn Bangerter, sister of Johnny Bangerter, was not raised in the Aryan Nations, but she watched her beloved older brother become entrenched in white power beliefs. After their mother and father had divorced, they moved from a predominantly white neighborhood in Utah to Las Vegas with their mother and were often involved in rumbles at school that always seemed to develop along racial lines. Statistics show that many girls join gangs for protection, especially when they've been sexually or otherwise harassed. Having a close family member get sucked up into the Movement sparked Lynn's devotion. She remembers the first time Johnny wore a swastika onstage singing with his heavy metal band. She told reporters, "It just felt right." She became convinced that he was following "the correct path." Their racist beliefs soon became their religion and a way of life.

Lynn once described the women's roles as vital to the Movement. "We make the banners and stuff, we make the food, and most important, we make the babies. As you know, the hand that rocks the cradle rules the world!" Lynn's assumption is correct in that women often take the responsibility for teaching the next generation of adults by greatly influencing who and what they turn out to be. That's why Johnny, Lynn, and her mother homeschooled all the local Aryan children. They would teach them their peculiar form of "Christianity" and other beliefs they thought were paramount to good, Aryan families. It's racism—family style—creating an intolerant view of other people, races, ethnic groups, and so forth. Most Aryan families homeschool their children to preserve them from "mongrel ideas."

For example, when talking about "outsiders," Lynn says, "I don't want to see them in cowboy hats and dancing in line dances. That just wouldn't look right. We all know it. Blacks, Asians . . . I have no problem with letting them go back to where they came from."

"And what if they don't want to go back to where they came from?" a reporter asked her once.

"Then I have a problem with that," she said sternly. When she and her brother Johnny speak violently about blacks, Jews, and the government, what are their children and the other children they influence supposed to grow up believing in, except fanatical racism?

Aryans also work governmental systems to the tee. For example, when Nicole and I were not yet legally married, she joined a group of Aryan girls and attended classes on how to effectively work the welfare system. Everyone in the Movement thought this was a great idea, not a disgrace. As much as we would all bitch about the blacks and Hispanics and race traitorous white and mongrel trash that were on the system, we felt *justified*. Of course, we weren't white trash, we were sucking money from the system that we had hated, and we rationalized that it would help to bring it down by burdening it even further.

Most Aryan girls would lie, saying that they didn't know who the father was, and the court never forced DNA tests. However, my name was on the birth certificates of my boys, so Nicole couldn't say that. Instead, she told a different story.

"My boyfriend lives with me," she had told the social worker, "but he keeps food separate from me and the kids." Welfare gave her $690 a month in cash, plus $300 to $400 in food stamps. That way, we used government money for rent and utilities, and all the money I made was for whatever we wanted to do. Everyone worked the system that way. It was easy justification for the girls to use, and of course it made it better for the men. The more kids we had, the more welfare would pay—and we loved that it would pay for all of our kids and contribute to that inevitable breakdown of society we were prepared to take advantage of.

Aryan girls ingeniously come up with ways to support their families without having to work. In California, they created the AWL, the Aryan Women's League. They would send out flyers, however, calling themselves the *American* Women's League.

"Please put out baby clothes, canned goods, furniture—anything you can donate to the needy," the flyers read. The girls would gather up truckloads of donated supplies—baby and children's clothing and food—and distribute it out to the different Aryan families. Sometimes a few shoddy items would be taken to the Salvation Army, but it was very rare that everything wasn't snatched up and used immediately by the Aryan mothers.

Another thing the women would teach was how to get on the government WIC program (Women with Infants and Children). In addition to welfare and the clothing drives, the WIC benefit paid for all the cheese, milk, eggs, diapers, and formula the babies needed so the money could go toward promoting our cause. It was an entirely effective system, which drew in a lot of girls involved in the Movement because they would teach it to poor and struggling white mothers to support them and their families. When these vulnerable girls showed up to receive assistance and learn from their new friends, a lot of them didn't have boyfriends. Since the Movement then was 90 percent guys, it was easy to hook up with one of the guys. Most of them had decent jobs, and perhaps treated them better than their last boyfriend. Once a man started taking care of a woman and her children, she often thought, *I should've been with this group all along.*

The women in Nicole's group in California also published coloring books and Aryan cookbooks. Once they compiled the books, they sold them online and in the *WAR* newspaper. Proceeds were often used to raise funds for POW wives. Since their boyfriends or husbands were in prison, the AWL supplied the stamps and letter-writing paper to keep the couples in contact with each other.

Hypocrisy was rampant within the ranks of women and men in the Movement. They were always making justifications for behaviors they made fun of other races for. For example, living off welfare, adultery, and abortion were considered off-limits activities that only other races should participate in, and yet members would often have justifications or excuses to utilize them for their own ends. Aryan dogma is that women should stand by their man and be strong and pure. However, in countless situations when the husbands were sent to jail for four or five years, the girls most often turned around and slept with other people. Aryan principles say they should be nurturers and caregivers, yet the girls were involved in as many knock-down, drag-out fights as the guys were. In many cases, women are the reason for much of the violence in and out of Aryan homes.

Aryan beliefs are often so dogmatic that other people generally felt uncomfortable around true Aryan women. Therefore the girls often want to stay at home and associate on the Internet or in small groups with other Aryans. They frequent Internet chat rooms and link up with other Aryan women and mothers so they do not feel alone in their beliefs. The women bring the ideologies into their homes in subtle and overt ways. Children and pets are often named symbolically, representing something important in the Aryan Movement. As with Nicole, many celebrate Hitler's birthday as more important than any other holiday of the year, and the women often make swastika cakes in celebration.

Aryan homes are filled with racist posters, confederate and swastika flags, books on Aryan and violent themes, and the women often wear clothing, tattoos, and jewelry with other insignias of hate.

These views are typical of the bigoted, racist ideals that run rampant in Aryan families. Those ideals are similar to the ones that ran rampant in my own small family until I saw how utterly devastating it could be for the future of my children—and even my children's children.

My own son Tommy would give a Nazi salute to any flag he saw. After all the gatherings and cross burnings and camps that Nicole and I had been to, he thought that was what all flags were for. That's what we had indoctrinated him with. The rhetoric, the violence, the hatred . . . Once I saw the Movement for what it really was, I wasn't proud of it. I knew what horrible futures my sons were destined for because of my mistakes. I knew I couldn't force them into any one direction, but I did feel that I should help to open their perspectives—to give them an *opportunity* to make a choice. You can't make a choice when it is all you know, but at least if you have the opportunity to see different sides to an equation, then you have the power to make a choice. I knew that's what my kids needed. Nicole has never agreed with me.

It got to the point though, once Julie and I were married, that the kids wanted to stay with us more often. We would often hear, "Why can't we stay with you this week?" In my opinion, it has been mostly positive because the boys have had the opportunity to establish a relationship with both their mom and their dad, which has been important to me. They have been able to see clearly inside two different kinds of worlds. Sometimes it has been hard on them, but I have taught the boys the importance of tolerance, even if you disagree with someone else's point of view. That became a painfully apparent lesson for Tommy.

Once his mother took him to a white power rally where there were hundreds of racists partying together. He got involved in a serious argument with a much older Skinhead who could have done a lot of damage to him. As the argument increased in intensity and ferocity, someone yelled at Nicole.

"Keep that kid's mouth shut or else!"

Fortunately, I believe that's the last rally she's taken him to.

22

TOLERANCE:
THE ONLY BANDAGE FOR THE
HATRED SORE

I BELIEVE THAT our country is SIC, or sick. We are sick because we are full of Silent, Indifferent, and Complacent people who think they don't have anything to do with gang problems and the violence in our society. Some people think ignoring intolerance, gangs, and racism will make it go away. It won't. Some people think if you sweep the streets clean of the gang bangers who are currently committing crimes and throw them all behind bars, the problem will be solved. It won't.

Gangs, like racism, have become inter-generational. They won't be stopped with one generation behind bars. There are too many younger brothers, sisters, and cousins out there with the same inherent beliefs about the world. In addition, prison gangs have become increasingly powerful and directly affects life on the streets. Racism and intolerance have become widespread in the cultures of our youth. It's in the music, the literature, the movies, the clothing—it's everywhere. Unfortunately, racism is made to look glamorous, rather than the cold, numb, and dark, guttural life it really is.

Prejudice is learned behavior, and so is tolerance. Who will teach our children tolerance? Interactive education about tolerance is the only key I've seen that will fit the lock of this problem. I believe education has to begin with kids as early as elementary age. As children progress into junior high and high school, this becomes even more critical. The entire community: parents, schools, law enforcement, courts, government, teachers, military, recreation centers, prisons, and businesses need to band together. As entities begin cooperating and collaborating together, we can begin to stem the tide of violence and intolerance. Educated adults can take an active part in the development and peaceful education of our youth.

Members of all gangs begin indoctrinating their young children as babies. Many Hispanic, black, white, Asian, and Russian gang members on the street are third and fourth generation, because they are educated *every day*! They are educated about politics, weapons, creating large and dangerous arsenals, drug running, prostitution, and controlling territory. They are educated in a cultural way that makes what they do accepted by their community—and makes everyone else the enemy.

Since leaving the Simon Wiesenthal Center, I have continued to spread the word about tolerance versus hate. I have continued to speak to law enforcement, schools, military, and educational institutions, and have made over five hundred appearances across the United States. While consulting is my business, teaching tolerance is my way of being.

I have been invited to visit several television programs, including the O'Reilly Factor, CNN, Nickelodeon, MTV, and the History Channel. I would love to see more public service announcements and more educational programs for kids. I found it interesting to be quoted in international magazines and newspapers, including Israeli, Russian, German, and Japanese. I've had the opportunity to meet the last two presidents of the United States, and then Governor Schwarzenegger. I was one of the guest speakers at the White House in Washington DC in a conference on hate crimes, and on the Governor's Advisory Panel on hate groups for Governor Gray Davis. In addition, I was on a national panel that included the Senior Assistant Attorney General, Southern Poverty Law Center, and the Simon Wiesenthal Center. I talked in front of a group of lawyers that were working for the governor at the time, along with educators, journalists, and law enforcement peace officers.

As I continue to work with law enforcement and to track gang activity around the United States and the globe, I realize that my ultimate vision to bring education, cultural acceptance, and tolerance is not something that will happen overnight. One of my favorite quotes is my philosophy: "I am only one, but because I am one, I will not stop doing what only I can do." I want others to raise the bar as well, and so I ask them, "What will you do that only you can do? How will you be your contribution?"

23

WHAT YOU DON'T KNOW CAN KILL

ANYONE WHO IS Jewish, black, Hispanic, Asian, homosexual, a government worker, or a tolerant white is the sworn enemy of Aryan Nations, who have vowed to annihilate the rest of society, one way or another. Their oath is as following:

"I, as an Aryan man, hereby swear an unrelenting oath upon the green graves of our sires, upon the children in the wombs of our wives, upon the throne of God almighty . . . to join together in holy union with those brothers in this circle and to declare forthright that from this moment on I have no fear of death, no fear of foe, that I have a sacred duty to do whatever is necessary to deliver our people from the Jew and bring total victory to the Aryan race. . . .

"My brothers, let us be His battle ax and weapon of war. Let us go forth by ones and twos, by scores and by legions, and as true Aryan men with pure hearts and strong minds face the enemies of our faith and our race with courage and determination.

"We hereby invoke the blood covenant and declare that we are in a full state of war and will not lay down our weapons until we have driven the enemy into the sea and reclaimed the land which was promised of our fathers of old, and through our blood and His will, becomes the land of our children to be."

Black, Mexican, Asian, Cuban, Puerto Rican, and even some Russian gangs have similar creeds. Loyalty only to the race, their race, and "blood-in, blood-out" which means a violent crime must be committed against an enemy to get jumped into a gang. The only way to leave is through natural death—or a violent death for those trying to escape the coils of the "brotherhood." Most gangs now force a swearing in for life, and they back their threats with the sting of death.

It doesn't help that American children are more afraid of local gang members than they are of the police. They know the power of gangs because they see it every day—from small power plays on the playground to vicious murders in their neighborhoods. They are learning *not* to come forward. They are also learning to be SIC—and theirs is the silence that begins the sickness.

Another disturbing fact is that there are now over five thousand hate sites on the Internet—a virtual playground for teens looking to fit into something. The White Aryan Resistance website reports it's had well over 11 million unique visitors since its birth. Just a few years ago, the FBI counted 256 hate groups in America. Today there are over 800 groups, with more yet to be identified. That's an alarming rate of growth for hatred and racism in the open and free country of America. Since many of these groups hate each other, many innocent people can and will get caught in the crossfire between the growing militant hate groups unless the silent American public takes a stand.

A couple of kids watching Pink Floyd's *The Wall* came up with an idea that became the biggest Skinhead gang of all time, Hammerskin Nation. Three years after I left the Movement, six Hammerskins attacked and repeatedly stabbed a young black man at an impromptu youth gathering, simply for the fact that he was black.

"We don't like niggers here!" "I hate niggers," "Die, nigger!" "Kill that nigger," and "We're going to get you, nigger," accompanied the assault with a bottle, screwdriver, razor knife, and folding knife. After the young teenager barely escaped to a stranger's home, the Skins were seen goose-stepping, giving Nazi salutes, and singing German songs. It is still happening. It still goes on.

Tom Metzger continues publicly teaching Skins to appear as normal citizens and operate covertly. At a 2004 Aryan Fest, Tom said, "The cause is best served by going underground. The government is becoming more oppressive. Our opponents are quite powerful." Metzger refers to himself as a white exterminist, rather than a separatist. Around Skinheads he wears provoking shirts that say things like "Some people are alive simply because it's illegal to kill them." Metzger openly targets the government through national terrorism, which he calls freedom fighting. "Don't stockpile firearms," he tells Skinheads. "How many guns can you shoot at once, guys? Besides, I could brew up bigger weapons than guns in my kitchen." Metzger continues to urge his followers to direct their energies toward political targets rather than futile street violence.

I think it's important to remember that it only took a couple of men with a twisted idea to plan a tragic event now termed the Oklahoma City Bombing. I already mentioned the five sailors in Norfolk, Virginia, who were only a few components shy of creating a hydrogen bomb. We have to keep in mind that it only took six men in Germany to have a twisted idea that wasn't stopped until millions and millions had been murdered.

What you don't know *can* kill, and *has* killed in America already—neighbors, friends, family, law enforcement, and military officers . . . the list goes on.

While I was an active member in California, the Skins were behind more chaos than the cops or the headlines and the community even suspected. In fact, as I mentioned earlier, a race war was nearly instigated during the time of the LA Riots. People don't know how close we came to inciting an all-out race war. We honestly felt justified. Our minds were full of racist propaganda, and we were prepared to go in and literally wipe out other races. During the riots, we were equipped to go in, dressed as SWAT cops in matching gear. We were prepared to drive an official-looking van into black neighborhoods and indiscriminately begin blowing away blacks. We knew the ramifications of *that* being viewed across American television—the hate that would infect the country and spread quickly, like a virus. Without questioning, blacks would likely retaliate, then whites and Hispanics would retaliate against them, and no one could have stopped the escalation, at least not until irreparable damage was done. Fortunately, one man stopped the escalation before it started. Tom Metzger pulled the plug on the idea. We were ready to go in, but he said we didn't have enough soldiers—that it was a suicide mission. Despite the fact that mayhem and murder were what Skins stood for, we didn't go in. To many in the Movement, that's the day when Tom lost face with the cause. But what people don't realize now is that today Tom *does* have enough soldiers. There are people specifically placed to do a lot of damage and bring the country to chaos in a short period of time—the lone wolf way. Tom's White Aryan Resistance website boldly states: "Lone Wolves are EVERYWHERE! We are in your neighborhoods, financial institutions, police departments, military, social clubs, and schools."

"People would be extremely shocked if they knew where a lot of our people are at right now," said Tom in a television interview. "They're close to the power."

I'm not shocked, but I am worried. I've witnessed how complacent most people and government institutions are. People don't think terrorists within the United States are powerful enough to do any damage. How quickly we forget Oklahoma City. I know that if another riot were to occur in LA today, Tom would say, "Go for it!" He believes there is another chance, and he will be ready this time. He thinks if he can make the situation big enough and get as much media coverage as possible, people will have no choice but to join one side or the other. That's exactly what he and the White Power Movement want. Like the splits and factions that the SHARPs forced on Skins across the nation—the Movement wants to factionalize us against our neighbors, against our grocer, our Senator, against family members, if need be. They want to force us into choosing sides, and they plan for the violence to keep people separated permanently.

Other people with a little more knowledge wonder why law enforcement doesn't just bust the Movement. They wonder how people in the Movement can be so bold as to write, "It can be dangerous to be right when the Government is wrong," and "There is hope with a scope." Part of it is because the Movement has gotten smart. Just like in prison, the Movement has leaderless "cell structures"—resistance warriors with no more than eight members. When they grow, they split off, so one group can't take another one down. Just because law enforcement can bust one cell doesn't mean they can bust another one. Most cells are very quiet. The Southern Poverty Law Center estimates that more than 750 white power organizations are active in the United States, the most notorious being the Klan, Aryan Nations, National Alliance, Hammerskins, and White Aryan Resistance. Most of them don't advertise how many there are in their memberships. They operate quietly, covertly.

There are a few hotheads who run around and say things publicly that get the attention they want and keep the Movements ideology somewhat public. Police are more careful about identifying dangerous situations and people after dealing with the aftermath of Timothy McVeigh and others. For example, a guy named Mahon from Arizona purported quite publicly (except when questioned by the police) to have hung out with McVeigh before the Oklahoma City Bombing. A little drunk and reckless, he described his ideals at a hate concert in the desert, and his comments were picked up in an investigative report by the *Phoenix New Times* and anyone else within earshot. "Terrorism works," said Mahon. "We did a lot of terrorism in Tulsa in the 1980s. We put heads in the road, and people paid attention. You have to give it to the Iraqis; they're putting us to shame right now. I mean, I hate those towel heads, but they're showing us how it's done." Mahon and another local Skin were blithely discussing how to get their hands on a Titan missile to destroy the nation's capital. "You nuke DC, you're going to wipe out most of the politicians, plus a couple million crack-head niggers," he said, and the other Skinhead agreed eagerly with him.

At that same concert, another leader of the Movement, Billy Joe Roper, then a thirty-one-year-old son of a Klansman, declared himself chairman of White Revolution. He says he's prepared to die or go to prison if need be to stop what he calls the amalgamation of America. In his opinion, mass genocide is preferable to race mixing. These are the kinds of people who live the words they speak to a dangerous level, and they are influencing many of America's children—our children.

We're seeing kids as young as eleven getting caught up into the doctrine of the Movement. Our society has witnessed graphic displays of violence by kids who are aligning with this dangerous ideology. Jeff Weise, the student who was implicated in the Red Lake Reservation school shootings in Minnesota, appears to have been a big fan of Adolf Hitler. He professed admiration for him and posted all sorts of messages on racist and anti-Semitic websites. He was obviously disturbed enough to commit a crime so heinous as to mirror the Columbine High School murders in Colorado. In fact, he played Columbine re-enactment video games. He bought into the hate rhetoric so heavily he actually perpetrated hate crimes against his own kind.

In 1995, heavy metal, punk, and hard-core music turned to hate, and a new kind of music was born. Resistance Records, a racist record label started in Detroit, began making money hand-over-fist. Other record labels have figured this out. The United States is the only nation in the world that can produce white power music legally—the *only* nation in the world. Bands from overseas come here to produce CDs that they can take back home and sell.

Panzerfaust Records created a cutting edge CD especially for kids in the United States, after a scheme entitled *Project Schoolyard* was thwarted in Germany when authorities learned of it. Panzerfaust claimed the CD was designed "to be inconspicuous and not racial so that it will fly below the radar screen of teachers and other people." Hmmm, not "overly racial," it included names like "Hate Train Rolling," "Under the Hammer," "Tales of Honor," "Commie Scum," "Thirst for Conquest," "American Justice," "White Supremacy," "Parasite," and "Might is Right," written by groups like H8Machine, Bound for Glory, Brutal Attack, Midtown Boot Boys, Rebel Hell, Day of the Sword, Aggressive Force, and Skrewdriver. Still, Byron Calvert, co-manager of Panzerfaust Records, remarked that "phase one of Project Schoolyard USA is complete. It was thought it would take at least two months to distribute the first batch of twenty thousand copies of the sampler CD. It took them two weeks." Imagine, twenty thousand hate-filled CDs on the street within two weeks. That is frighteningly efficient.

In addition, white power record labels are producing MTV-style videos to download online. There are also white power radio stations online who offer podcasts. Any kid with an iPod and picture capability can download pornography into their iPod, and the same is true of full graphic videos, repeating hate themes, and ugly threats against Jews. I think it's very telling in our society that the very first people to embrace new technology are pornographers and racists.

Some video games have become graphically motivating to kill Jews, blacks, homosexuals, and so forth. The object of the popular game, *Ethnic Cleansing*, is to kill as many blacks and Hispanics as possible until the Master Jew can be found, hiding in the subway. Once he is annihilated, the game is won. There are also patches that go with benign games such *PacMan*, turning them into violent, racial killing games.

Magazines and newsletters are effective tools to bring in new blood to the Movement, and they even have those tailored to kids and teens. Gorgeous girls on the glossy covers and on the inside spread give the message that girls are looking for Aryan men. The more girls there are, the more guys come into the Movement. Slick comic books and coloring books also promote the new world order through the use of "White Will"—a stalwart and seemingly brave racist character—and are made to be appealing to young audiences.

Neo-Nazis and white supremacists are not in the United States alone. We live in a country that makes it possible for subversives to voice their violent opinions somewhat non-violently. However, this is a problem and a challenge throughout the world. Many people don't realize that in the UK, for instance, *ten* separate British organizations have been described as neo-Nazi. These include:

- The British Movement
- The British National party
- The British Nazi party (the November 9th Society)
- The International Third Position
- The National Front
- The National Socialist Movement (linked to London nail bomber David Copeland)
- The NF Flag Group
- League of St. George
- Combat 18
- The White Nationalist party

There are also separatists and neo-Nazis in Russia, Scandinavia, France, Belgium, Malta, Canada, Brazil, Romania, Australia, New Zealand, Latvia, Iran, and many, many other nations. The threat is real.

As a nation, as a global society, our children simply are not safe until they know the history of the destructive power of hate, what it continues to do, and what it could bring to our great nation if it is not healed by tolerance. They deserve to develop critical thinking habits, to see for themselves what works and what doesn't, and to be taught the benefits of tolerance and peaceful solutions to community and world problems.

We are seeing the emergence of a huge issue in the United States and Europe—immigration. While immigration has always been a sticky point in politics, the Movement is using the rifts in society to plant seeds of further discord and disharmony. If separatists can get the average, everyday worker to feel that life is unfair—that they are being "jipped" or "jewed" out of their rightful place in the workforce, if they can get people to get angry about the amount of non-whites on welfare that their tax dollars are going to support, they can get people involved in a race war. That's what the people behind the Movement want. Americans for peace need to be aware of this, ready for this, educated about this, and teach our children about this. Tolerance is natural to a young child, but even after cultural and family norms of bigotry, racism, or hatred set in, tolerance can still be *taught*. Perspectives can still be opened.

Some people have asked me how I can remain so passionate about what I do. They think I've given enough back to society, I've changed my life, and why not move on to a more lucrative field? There are many reasons, positive and negative, that keep me motivated.

A few years ago, after giving a talk to high school students in a town in California, a mother came up to speak with me. I could tell my talk had touched her deeply. Still, there was something else in her eyes. She was quite emotional.

"I wish my son could have heard you speak," she said to me, tears beginning to flow, "but now it's too late."

"What is your son's name?" I asked her. When she mentioned his first name, it didn't strike me, but as soon as I heard his last name, bells went off in my head. I recalled that her son was one of several WHS members who had just been sentenced to four years in prison for a hate crime. My heart fell, and I understood why she was feeling so emotional. I also knew why my heart was pounding in my chest.

"I am so sorry for what I have done to you and your family," I said, choking back tears of my own.

"It wasn't your fault," she replied. "You hadn't ever met him, had you?"

"No, I didn't know him," I said, my heart still heavy. "However, he was recruited by one of the kids that I recruited. He was brought into the Movement because of me." This moment painfully illustrated how my legacy of hate continues, even as some of my former friends are still recruiting. This story and countless others is one of the driving forces that keep me going. As much as I would like to change the past, I cannot, so I continue to look at the good I can do right now—how I can inspire others to move from a life of destruction and hate to a life of creativity and contribution. I have to look at the forty-one kids I've been able to get *out* of the Movement and out of the misery of gang life. I look at them and know that they also continue to ripple, affecting friends, family, and associates in a positive way. How many lives are they touching for good? How many people are they saving from a fifteen-year mistake? This is why I am so passionate about moving forward in this work.

"And because I am one, I will not stop doing what only I can do." If someone as pig-headed and intolerant as I used to be can learn tolerance, *anyone* can. I have great faith in our children, our nation, and our global community. Miracles are possible.

APPENDIX

Glossary of Racist Terms, Acronyms, and Hate Codes

RACIST TERMS

Bonehead: SHARPs' term used for racist Skinheads.

Boot Party: When a group of Skinheads commit a violent assault.

Bootboy: Another name for Skinhead.

Braces: Another name for suspenders. Worn down indicates readiness for a fight.

Brother: A term used to refer to another racist.

Brotherhood: A term racists use when referring to a group of Aryan men, or to their own group.

Chelsea/Renee/Fringe/Feathercuts: A term for a Skinhead girl's hairstyle.

Crew/Club: Another name for gang.

Crop: The term Skinheads use for short hair.

Docs/Boots: Another name for Dr. Martens boots.

Fag Bashing: Refers to an attack on a homosexual.

Flights: The name Skinheads use for military jackets.

Fred Perry: A brand of polo shirt Skinheads wear.

Fresh Cut/Boot: Another name for a new Skinhead.

Hunting: A term for a night out looking for someone to attack.

Kike: A derogatory term for a member of the Jewish faith.

Lop: Refers to a person that is of no use.

Mud/Mud Races/Subhuman: Refers to all non-white or minorities.

Mud Shark: A term Skinheads use for a white female who dates non-whites/minorities.

OI!: A Skinhead way of saying, hello or good-bye.

Prospect/Probate: A term used for someone who wants to be a Skinhead but still needs to prove himself.

Put in Check/Schooling/Rough Justice: When older Skinheads attack younger Skinheads to teach them a lesson.

Race Traitor: A white person who associates with non-whites, minorities, or Jews.

Skin: Short for Skinhead

Toad: A term Skinheads use for blacks.

Two-Tone/Trojans: A term Skinheads use for SHARPs.

Wigger: A term used by racists to describe white people who are acting black in their eyes (white nigger).

Wood: Short for Peckerwood

ACRONYMS

ACAB: All Cops Are Bastards

AKIA: A Klansman I Am

AN: Aryan Nation

FTW: Forever Truly White

HBH: Heil Blood Honour

HFFH: Hammerskin Forever, Forever Hammerskin

ITSUB: In The Sacred Unfailing Bond

KLASP: Klannish Loyalty A Sacred Principle

ORION: Our Race Is Our Nation

-P-: Symbol used in e-mail and on web boards, meaning Phinehas Priesthood

RAC: Rock Against Communism

RaHoWa/ROHOWA: Racial Holy War

ROA: Race Over All (used only by Volksfront)

SANBOG: Strangers Are Near, Be On Guard

SHARP: Acronym for Skinhead Against Racial Prejudice.

SWP: Supreme White Power

WAR: White Aryan Resistance

WCOTC: World Church Of The Creator

WP: White Power or White Pride

WPWW: White Pride World Wide

ZOG: Zionist Occupational Government (Jewish controlled)

HATE CODES

A=1   B=2   C=3   D=4   E=5   F=6   G=7   H=8   I=9

8/H: Hate

88/HH: Heil Hitler (used as a greeting or good-bye by a racist)

18/AH: Adolf Hitler

58/EH: Extreme Hatred

83/HK: Haken Kreuz: German for *swastika*

83/HC: Heil Christ: Used by racist Christian groups

5 Words: I have nothing to say

16/AF: American Front

816: Heil American Front

28: Blood and Honour

828/HBH: Heil Blood and Honour

228/BBH: Brotherhood Blood and Honour

38: Crossed Hammers

386: Crossed Hammers Forever

311 or 3/11: Ku Klux Klan

14 Words: We must secure the existence of our people and a future for white children.

14 Words for Women: Because the beauty of the white Aryan woman must not perish from the Earth.

55/HF—FH: Hammerskins Forever—Forever Hammerskin

H/8 F/6 8+6 = 14: Now if you break down 14, 1+4 = 5

Black Laces: Black laces are worn by fresh cuts. These laces are used by new Skinheads who have not earned their white laces.

White Laces: White pride or white power. It also shows that someone has earned the right to be called a Skinhead.

Red Laces/Blood Laces: Show that a Skinhead has drawn serious blood, i.e., an attempted murder or murder.

Yellow or Gold Laces: These are also used by Skinhead to symbolize Anarchy, while other Skinheads have used this color to signify an assault of a law enforcement officer.

PICTURES

My mother and father while dating in 1965.

In 1981, when I was fifteen years old, in the backyard of my uncle's house at a party. I had already started getting into the Skinhead Movement.

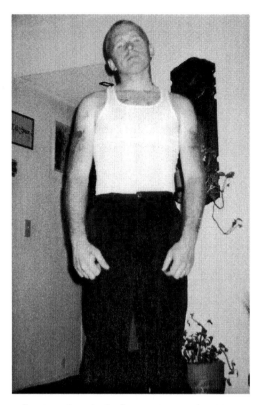

January of 1988, shortly before entering the Marine Corps.

Hammerskin party, shortly after the founding of
Western Hammerskins in 1989.

Visitors' Sunday at the Marine Corps Recruit Depot in San Diego, April
1988, when Phil, my mom, Renee, and my dad came to see me.

On leave in August of 1989, when I became the enforcer
for the Hammerskins.

Swastika lighting at Aryan Fest in Tulsa Oklahoma in 1989,
while I was in the Marines.

A mosh pit at Aryan Nations in April of 1995 during the annual
conference, which purposefully coincides with Hitler's birthday.

The SS bolts and the soldier represent a person who is committed to the armed struggle. These were earned by a stabbing.

Iron Eagle tattoo earned for a racial altercation.

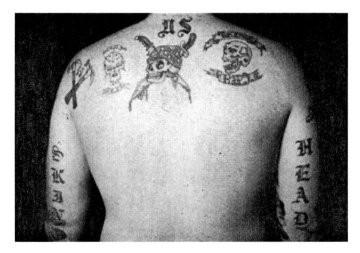

The original Western Hammerskins logo on the left shoulder, given when I joined.

Tommy giving a Nazi salute at Aryan Nation's world conference in 1995.

Konrad standing in front of racist posters at the world conference in 1995.

Tommy and Konrad in May of 1996 at a park in Longview, Washington, about fifteen minutes before I had to surrender them back to the custody of their mother, because the court ordered it.

George W. Bush, the first year he took office in 2001. We were discussing my transformation and what I was doing since then for the Simon Wiesenthal Museum.

Then actor, now governor, Arnold Schwarzenegger at a benefit dinner at the Simon Wiesenthal Center in 1997.

Julie and I, taken at a friend's birthday party shortly after we were first married.

Julie and I, taken at our home in 2006.

0 26575 51333 2